The Role ⟨

In A

Operations Excellence Transformation

Model

Darrell L. Casey, Ph.D.

ISBN 978-0-557-00425-6

PUBLISHERS NOTE

The following book is the finalized product of Dr. Casey's research

and dissertation to fulfill requirements leading the Doctor of

Philosophy degree in Business Administration in 2005. As such, it is

a reprint of the original published dissertation and the reader should

note the formalized format supports criteria outlined by the American

Psychological Association *Publication Manual.*

Since his original publishing, Dr. Casey has finalizing and prepared for

publication in late 2008 the following book:

Transforming
Traditional Lean Paradigms
Into
Distinctive Enterprise Competencies

Darrell L. Casey, Ph.D.

Peoria, IL

© 2008

And the forthcoming book publication in 2009:

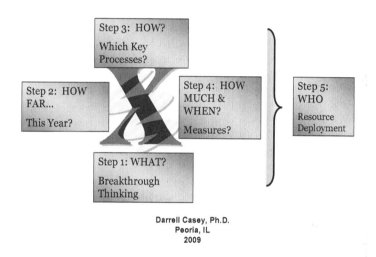

Strategic Deployment X Matrix Process

Step 3: HOW? Which Key Processes?

Step 2: HOW FAR... This Year?

Step 4: HOW MUCH & WHEN? Measures?

Step 5: WHO Resource Deployment

Step 1: WHAT? Breakthrough Thinking

Darrell Casey, Ph.D.
Peoria, IL
2009

ABSTRACT

While world markets continue to heat up with brutal competition, interest in *Operations Excellence* strategies will either be embraced by businesses or they will be left behind in the dust of their competitors. Current strategic models attempt to drive successful implementation through a project approach focused only upon the specific techniques required to yield rapid high impact results. This singular piecemeal approach fails to develop and mature into distinctive competencies required for sustainable competitive advantage.

Operations excellence therefore must be an organization transformation initiative in which change leadership roles are a crucial set of characteristics necessary for overall success. The achievement of distinctive competencies is rooted in the developmental maturity of; strategy execution, organizational structures, enterprise processes and culture. These distinctive competencies are lacking in the majority of previous businesses attempts; hence the high level of failure. Initiative failure in traditionally managed organizations stems from the foundational lack of change leadership that; creates a shared vision, communicates for understanding, sets new expectations, creates a sense of urgency, leads by example, holds all individuals accountable, follows up and rewards desired behaviors - thereby establishing the new culture.

To achieve sustainable competitive advantage is not simply the deployment of techniques of lean manufacturing, but the creation of distinctive competencies within business resources. Distinctive competencies built upon performance results based in knowledge, expectations, behaviors, and standards of performance; hence the culture of operations excellence.

TABLE OF CONTENT

LIST OF TABLES

CHAPTER ONE: INTRODUCTION

Introduction

Richard Draft (2001) in *Organization Theory and Design* declares:

> Organizations must run fast to keep up with changes taking place all around them. Organizations must modify themselves not just from time to time, but all of the time... Today's organizations must poise themselves to innovate and change, not only to prosper but merely to survive in a world of increased competition. Organizations that invest most of their time and resources in maintaining the status quo cannot hope to prosper in today's world of constant change and uncertainty. (p.352)

Change, as noted in the opening quote, is a requirement simply for survival today and is essential to business longevity for the future. As world markets continue to heat up with competition, interest in *Operations Excellence* strategies will either be embraced or the business will be left behind in the dust of their competitors who sped by on a fast pace to profits and revenue growth. Businesses have taken heed and through the previous decade of the nineties and into the initial years of the twenty first century have begun to position themselves for the highly competitive environment by implementing various strategies targeting increased profits and productivity. A great percentage of these companies will launch initiatives identified to include operations excellence strategies focused upon efforts to reduce not only cost but lead time to customers while decreasing the amount of defects, thereby gaining a competitive advantage. Strategies such as this are rooted in the aspects offered through implementation of *Lean Manufacturing*.

Fixation on shorter lead times, rapid product launches, higher quality levels, and enhanced productivity lead companies to benchmark themselves to Toyota. In their quest to drive superior performance improvements companies cite Toyota's competitive advantage based entirely upon techniques such as *Kanban, Single Minute Exchange of Dies (SMED), Just In Time (JIT), Total Productive Maintenance (TPM)*, etc.

This intense focus has been heighten through multitudes of books written on these various topics and marketed as the tools that drove the *Toyota Production System (TPS)* and other world class businesses to their competitive advantage. Reinforcing these concepts, consultants align themselves to the same premise catering services to businesses with promises of greater profits and revenue growth through the implementation of these same techniques as used by Toyota.

Nevertheless, as the world class benchmark, Toyota has no fear of losing its competitive position. The company provides tours of its operations to numerous business executives, engineers, and professional personnel, many representing direct competitors of Toyota. Yet, Toyota's leadership realize that the result of these tours are individual questions about specific lean techniques and the single minded focus on results gained through their implementation; not how did Toyota's create the operations excellence culture – the foundation of sustainable competitive advantage.

Competitive advantage in the market can come from a new product, service, or processes; however these are short lived due to reproducibility by competitors. True competitive advantage that is sustainable comes from the organizational resources and their capabilities. Operations excellence requires moving beyond the specific techniques of lean manufacturing typically associated with incremental improvement (Kaizen) and taking implementation to a level of breakthrough.

Breakthrough operations excellence is radical change that transforms the entire organization (Figure 1) including; strategic leadership, focused and aligned structure, improved holistic processes, execution excellence, control systems with meaningful metrics and performance expectations. These become the supporting mechanism to new expectations, values and beliefs executed by leadership that leverage organizational capabilities into a new culture. Organizational capabilities that are founded upon human and intangible assets providing superior performance and nearly impossible to reproduce by competitors; thereby creating distinctive competencies.

Prior to implementation of an operations excellence strategic initiative it must be clearly understood that to gain a competitive advantage, the business must move beyond the traditional incremental application of techniques for rapid high impact results. The business must embrace a culture driven by both incremental and breakthrough changes that provide enhanced performance through efficiency of processes as well as sustained effectiveness of resources based on new organizational expectations, behaviors and standards of excellence.

The list of industry and business is full of examples having undergone the implementation of specific aspects of operations excellence. Nevertheless, from this list, the majority ended in failure or at best partial implementations; a minority of organizations have succeeded to a level of declared competitive advantage. Industry surveys show that nearly two thirds of strategic implementations by businesses end in failure. Yet, traditionally managed companies continue to attempt implementation in a fashion that cherry picks only the aspects of interest for anticipated fast bottom line results. Following the leads from prominent consultants, best selling books, and expensive seminars that tout the benefits of various lean manufacturing techniques companies embark upon the operations excellence journey. Implementation takes on a narrow scoped single event approach, focused only in one specific functional area and conducted in project management style with a start and end date versus a structured approach built upon the creation of system wide changes through a never ending cycle of adaptation.

Vital to this later condition is the active commitment by leadership that is outwardly expressed in every daily role such as projection of vision, constant communication through multiple media form, personal example of the new expected behaviors, and reinforcement through feedback methods. However, as the numbers indicate, typically companies proceed with a poorly planned functional approach that in some instances gains an improved level of performance for a short period of time. But focus shifts, interest in the specific accomplishment wanes, individuals are transferred, or no follow up commitment and feedback methods are in place, so within a short span of time the success regresses back to the old method and status quo. The exact traditional approach that Toyota has learned poses no threat to their competitive position.

To compete in today's economy against world class business requires breakthrough strategies that create winning organizational cultures that become the very fabric of the business; system wide breakthrough that transforms structure, processes, and control methods thereby creating a new culture. Not incremental focused events targeting technical aspects for the rapid fix or result and fail to modify resource capability and behaviors. Caution must be used to ensure that the overall strategy is not to set out to change the culture, but to focus and align changes through combining the efficiencies associated with lean manufacturing with the effectiveness derived through new standards, norms, behaviors, and expectations so culture change is a natural occurrence supporting overall business strategy.

This approach provides the transformation of resources that are capable of sustaining the competitive advantages gained. As Robert S. Kaplan and David P. Norton (2001) provide in their book, *The Strategy Focused Organization: How Balanced Scorecard Companies Thrive in the New Business Environment:*

> Clearly, opportunities for creating value are shifting from managing tangible assets to managing knowledge – based strategies that deploy an organization's intangible assets: customer relationships, innovative products and services, high quality and responsive operating processes, information technology and databases, and employee capabilities, skills, and motivation. (p. 2)

Problem Statement

With global competition at such a dynamic level that any day lost without operations improvement imperials the company's economic position, status quo simply leads to failure. Too out pace this competitive environment, companies are implementing strategies to establish competitive advantage as a low cost producer or as a stand out through product differentiation. The overall strategic intent is the creation of systems with resources that are capable, flexible, and reliable to a performance level that establishes distinctive competencies in quality, efficiency, innovation, and responsiveness. This distinctive competency thereby establishes greater value for both the customer and shareholders. One of most prominent methods many companies are currently choosing to create these distinctive competencies is operations excellence; specifically through the application of lean manufacturing.

The choice of operations excellence as a strategic initiative to create competitive advantage signals the confidence executives have placed in the ability to achieve cost reductions, reduced lead-times, and improved quality. For many companies, the need for improvement is beyond mere competitive to that of simple survival. Businesses must realize that the time, effort, and assets utilized to implement operations excellence can be disastrous to the overall business if the initiative leads to failure.

Today, most companies have an understanding of the various techniques associated with lean manufacturing that has been gained through a multitude of books, seminars, and consulting expertise available. Nevertheless, industrial benchmarks reflect that nearly two thirds of operations excellence implementations fail. With all the techniques and methods available "why have so many failed at this strategic endeavor?" Finding the business in a position of basic survival and loss of competitive edge, company executives embark upon strategic initiatives to improve cost structures and grow revenue. In the rush to make something happen, traditional strategic methodology is used with a narrow scope of approach, lack of understanding, lack of planning, and more importantly, lack of change leadership required to achieve competitive advantage.

The strategy of choice is either major cost reductions in order to be the low cost producer, or product differentiation via quality and services provided. Management expectation is to drive the strategy from corporate down to individual operations, linked only to traditional tangible business metrics in hope to secure rapid impact. In order to achieve the rapid results desired, individual operations turn to the various opportunities promised through implementation of lean manufacturing techniques. However, based on existing traditional models, execution relies heavily upon the application of specific lean techniques through single events leading to simple incremental improvement in efficiency providing one time cost reductions or productivity gains.

Characteristically, information gathered during benchmarking, review of industry best practices, or the enthusiasm to gain advantages similar to Toyota reinforces managements desire to utilize operations excellence as the strategy of choice. In many causes market conditions have placed the business in a corner from which rapid cost reductions are seen as the only course of action to protect shareholder value. Traditional management finds it easier to reduce headcount for productivity and profitability than the creation of greater market share or new innovative capabilities that increase return on investment.

In this scenario, management selects a few areas that promise the greatest impact through cost reductions, productivity gains, quality improvement, etc. Then to head up this new program, a manager is assigned based upon a track record of achievement and getting things done fast. Normally, the approach is project management style coupled with command and control. This traditional model is concerned with the implementation of technical solutions, gaining results, and moving on to the next firefight. Little or no concern is given to the "soft" aspects of implementation such as organization development and cultural leadership.

Typically, the launching of the initiative is accomplished with great fanfare with announcements that the company is launching operations excellence, a mass meeting is held to tell employees, banners, coffee mugs, polo shirts are handed out, all in the thought that the employees will step right up with full commitment and ownership of the endeavor. Nonetheless, the employees are skeptical at best, moan that it's another flavor of the day program, or read right through the situation and see that no matter what the company calls the program - it comes down to cost reductions.

After months of planning and leading specific Kaizen events the company finds itself no closer to the high impact results desired while corporate management is applying greater pressure for performance improvements, countermeasures, and additional resources to get on track. The project manager, usually given the title of Lean Manufacturing Manager commensurate with his or her level in the operation is working diligently at identifying and applying the various techniques. True to the traditional models, the project is in a very specific area, with a demanding top down focus on the application of a selected technique used to reduce cost with minimal operator involvement. Many times there is little or no planning and the whole perspective is that of treating the initiative as a single event or at best a series of disjointed events.

The small gains that are achieved can not be sustained by the workforce assigned in the area since they were not involved, have no set expectations, and are not monitored for performance. Many times, with the abundance of daily management issues and firefighting activities, the direction of the project manager is re-focused to another area of the operation removing the source of knowledge, individual pacesetter, and daily management attention permitting the improvement changes to regress back to old norms. Little or no time is spent on the organizational change leadership aspects so vital to creating the new values, expectations, standards and behaviors that support sustainable change.

The sustainable competitive advantage strategy for operations excellence was revolutionized by Toyota with the concept of lean manufacturing commonly referred to as TPS. For many years, Toyota has opened its doors allowing tours of their manufacturing operations to direct and non- direct competitors. Yet, through these years Toyota has not had a fear of loss of competitive advantage by providing these tours and permitting competitors to see specific operations and methods.

Toyota has been able to remain secure in the knowledge that their operations excellence is built upon organizational culture and resource capability, true distinctive competencies not the simple techniques of lean manufacturing. Unfortunately, these techniques are the repeated focus of attention and questions by traditional tour participants in search of fast results and bottom line impacts; not how or what change leadership and organizational development aspects created the sustainable competitive advantage. Toyota's sustainable competitive advantage is secure in the fact that participants will not ask about, will overlook, or have failed to recognize the importance of culture, change leadership, and organization transformation.

Current traditional business and strategic models attempt to drive implementation of operations excellence through events focused on the specific techniques of lean to yield rapid high impact results. This model fails to develop and mature resource capabilities into distinctive competencies required for sustained competitive advantage. Operations excellence therefore must be an organization transformation initiative in which change leadership roles are a crucial set of characteristics of overall success. The achievement of distinctive competencies will be rooted in the development and maturity of organizational structures, processes, and culture that has been lacking in a majority of previous transformations attempts leading to the high level of failure.

Root cause of initiative failure in a traditionally managed organization stems from the fundamental lack of change leadership. Lack of a clear understanding that implementation of sustainable operations excellence is not simply about deploying techniques of lean manufacturing, but about the creation of distinctive competencies in the business resources. Resource capabilities built upon knowledge, establishment of new values, expectations, behaviors and standards of performance, as well as alignment of the organizational structure coupled with process improvement to support the new strategy. The real bottom line realization is that sustainable competitive advantage through operations excellence is only achievable through organizational transformation.

Purpose of the Study

The research provided in the following documentation will identify, set forth, and develop the factors of change leadership which create successful operations excellence transformation. To establish their selves as low cost producer or product differentiator an increasing numbers of businesses are seeking operations excellence so as to develop superior performance in quality, innovation, cost, and customer responsiveness. Typically, these businesses look to process and product improvement techniques to drive their competitive advantage. Yet, to ensure sustainability of the competitive advantage gained, operations excellence must be implemented in a system wide, holistic approach leading organization transformation in structures, processes, and culture creating distinctive competencies in resources.

Businesses fail to realize that to gain true competitive advantage that is sustainable, implementation must transform the organization with resources and culture that is capable of adaptation and learning. Therefore, operations excellence models need to create a focus and alignment within the organization that develops and matures resource capability into distinctive competencies. This goes beyond the existing models that utilize an approach of simple one time execution of specific techniques of lean manufacturing by replacing these with a new model built upon breakthrough improvements associated with transformation.

Breakthroughs that include the establishment of an organization structure that supports and aligns to operations excellence, processes throughout the business that create ownership at the applicable levels while fostering experimentation and learning for best practice. These are coupled with overall performance feedback and reward systems that measure the appropriate metrics that have meaning and reinforce desired behaviors. Competitive advantage that is sustainable therefore becomes heavily involved in organization wide change taking implementation from the technical "hard stuff" to a major undertaking of the "soft stuff."

The high level of failure to successfully implement a sustainable competitive advantage in operations excellence leads to the need for identification of the reasons why, as well as establishing criteria for change leadership that fosters favorable outcomes so that organizational culture is transformed. This study will identify elements that lead to failure, and outline fundamental change leadership roles with organizational culture change essentials which must be present in a new model for leadership of operations excellence transformation.

Importance of the Study

Strategies of low cost producer and product differentiation such as quality, innovation, efficiency, and customer responsiveness are vital aspects required of all businesses in global competition. The ability of a business to create resources that are capable, flexible, and reliable provides an unbeatable distinctive competency. Yet, with so much competitive position riding upon successful operations excellence, industry surveys conclude that nearly two thirds of the companies in such endeavors fail in the initiative.

As businesses find themselves outpaced by competitors in certain areas such as lead time, productivity or reliability, and armed with technical solutions of lean manufacturing, they have rushed to begin efforts to improve performance by announcing that the organization will move forward with a new strategic initiative in one or several selected organization areas. However, months and even years after beginning the task a large majority of these business are still struggling with the implementation of techniques, have not achieved the desired and expected results or have given up pursuit of the objective due to difficulty in gaining lasting outcomes.

In many of these companies, management entered the initiative with thoughts that the techniques of lean manufacturing could be implemented within an established timeline and results forthcoming through improved performance in quality, lead time, and reduced cost structures. Initial deployments typically yield some improved results, but after a period of time these performance enhancements fall back to previous levels or obscurity. No matter how efficient the techniques, without effective deployment within the total organization there is a greater traditional culture counteracting the changes and seeking to return to previous standards and behaviors.

The appeal for operations excellence, specifically lean manufacturing, is reinforced dramatically from the high level of visibility in business and industry due to the multitudes of published books, articles, seminars, and numerous consulting experts that have specialized in various techniques. In turn, each technique has been expanded upon in their own right including detailed aspects of TPM, JIT, Kanban, SMED, etc. This multitude of books, seminars, and consulting expertise follows a traditional model focused on technical "hard" aspects and lacks an integrated approach to operations excellence. An approach that combines techniques with the two critical aspects of organizational culture change and change leadership that must occur for successful transformation. Simply put, the expertise misses the mark of "how" to implementing lean manufacturing.

The importance of this study is to identify the vital change leadership roles in the implementation of operations excellence as well as the corresponding efforts that must occur in the development and maturity of key organizational structures, processes, and controls to align behind the strategy. A new model will be proposed in the research that provides total integration of operations excellence so that the various techniques are supported by development of resource capabilities; a model that creates distinctive competencies within the business thereby creating sustainable competitive advantage.

Scope of the Study

The scope of this study will be in three main areas of:

1.   Examination of current operations excellence
         practices based upon traditional models for
         lean manufacturing, along with their reliance
         upon specific techniques for rapid results.
         Identification and defining of transformation
         requirements as well as criteria for change
         leadership to establish a successful
         organization environment and distinctive
         competencies.

2.   Surveys will be conducted via on-line links to
         participants in telecommunications,
         manufacturing, financial, and professional
         services. Data collected will be utilized to
         form the background of the research into
         current operations excellence strategic intent,
         the level of attainment and sustainability of
         performance results, identification of barriers
         to implementation, and determination of

perceived levels of change leadership success from senior managers compared to individuals within the workforce. This later battery of surveys will determine critical characteristics of change leadership roles.

3.   Research conducted via the surveys, one on one interviews, research of classical and contemporary experts in operations excellence and organizational culture, coupled with first hand experience will lead to a final conclusion. The outcome of the research is to create an Operations Excellence Transformation Model that integrates the basic lean manufacturing techniques with organizational culture and change leadership elements. One overall model that can be utilized by business leaders to establish sustainable competitive advantage through the transformation of the organization with distinctive competencies gained from lean manufacturing. This model

will provide key roles in proper phase

sequencing for maturity development.

Rationale of the Study

Operations excellence, specifically lean manufacturing

have been buzzwords of the 90's and early twenty first

century. While nearly all businesses are endeavoring towards

competitive position through operations excellence, many are

wasting valuable company time and resources that can never

be recovered if the strategic intent is not sustainable.

Organizations that have successfully embraced

operations excellence are not traditionally run organizations

that operate more efficiently than in the past. They are

organizations radically changed in structure, processes,

control methods that support superior performance in quality,

cost, innovations, and customer service. The dramatic

transformation from a traditionally ran operation to one of

excellence requires change leadership at all levels, from the

front office to shop floor. Breakthrough change in the

organizational culture that creates resources that are capable, flexible, and reliable; the distinctive competencies of business.

Many of today's managers are well versed in the definitions of lean manufacturing as well as various models of implementation. Nevertheless, industry surveys reflect that two thirds of businesses implementing operations excellence fail to achieve desired results of reduced cost, increase quality levels, and reduced lead time to customers. The difficulty of gaining the sustainable competitive advantage of operations excellence lies in the gap between knowing what lean is and truly understanding how to achieve it. Few traditional managers' posses more than a vague idea of the specific day to day change leadership activities that are required to create and sustain an operations excellence environment. Without this fundamental knowledge, efforts to establish an organization based on operations excellence is always marked with frustration, unfulfilled expectations, loss of market share, and profits.

Definition of Terms

The follow is a glossary of terms that are used throughout this study.

Breakthrough Change involves the entire organization in transformation

to new structures, processes, and control systems, typically creating a new culture.

Change is the process of dynamic growth and development for the organization, groups, and individual.

Competitive Advantage when a company's profitability and revenue

growth is greater than the average for all companies within its industry.

Culture the learned and shared assumptions of a group that produce predictable behavior and decisions.

Customer is both internal and external reception of the unit, the next step in the value stream.

Distinctive Competencies are unique strengths within the organization that allow the company to achieve a lower cost structure or differentiate its products and services from the competition. Since the distinctive competencies are unique within a business, they are established based on resources and capabilities.

Effectiveness examines how well an organization obtains its objectives and goals.

Efficiency is the amount of resources utilized in achievement of objectives and goals.

Empowered Teams are team structures within the operation that have

developed to a level at which management provides mentoring and coaching allowing the teams a high level of self leadership, responsibility and authority.

Excellence is a level of developmental maturity in which improvement

activities yield continuous successes.

Incremental Change represents single event improvements that are highly focused on a specific topic while maintaining the overall organizations structure, processes, and control systems.

Kaizen is continuous improvement through incremental improvements

Key Performance Indicators (KPIs) are metrics that have been identified as critical to measuring the overall performance of the operation.

Lead Time is the total time from start of the manufacturing system of raw material through to shipping of the product.

Lean is producing the maximum sellable products or services at the lowest operational cost while optimizing inventory levels.

Lean Manufacturing is a manufacturing philosophy using various

techniques to create effectiveness through increased flexibility, reliability, and

capability of resources while reducing or eliminating non value added activities.

Maturity is a level of organizational development in which improvement

activities yield more successes than failures.

Non Added Value is activities or actions taken that add no real value to the product or service, making such activities or actions a form of waste.

Operations Excellence is a level of process improvement which achieves

continuous successes in lower cost, higher quality, reduced lead time, and increased innovation.

Operation is an individual station, machine, that has specific assigned

work content or function to perform.

Policy Deployment also known as Strategy Deployment, is a process for the alignment and integration of initiatives, objectives, selection of goals, designation of people and resources for project completion and establishment of project metrics.

Process is the combination of operations or machines which complete a

specific set of functions or work content, example, paint process, assembly process, quality process, etc.

Plant Steering Team (PST) a guiding coalition comprised of functional champions as well as employee's throughout the plant. Team

provides executive communications, guidance, prioritize, and assign resources and initiatives.

Quality is the meeting expectations and requirements, stated and unstated of the customer.

Radical Change involves the entire organization in transformation to

new structures, processes, and control systems, typically creating a new culture.

Six Sigma methodology and techniques used to eliminate and or reduce variation in product or processes thereby increasing overall efficiency.

Strategic Intent is what you are working to accomplish.

System is the collection of process required to provide a completed deliverable unit or information, Example manufacturing system.

Transformation is a movement toward a future state or vision while creating a new standard.

Transformational Change is the process of becoming something different, something better.

Value Added is activities or actins taken that add real value to the product or service.

Vision is an outlook or created future state of operation which is

expressed to mobilize people, facilitate change and growth for the

organization.

Waste is anything that uses resources, but does not ad real

value to the product or service.

Overview of the Study

In today's global business environment companies can

not remain fixed in state of compliancy or satisfied in a

position of status quo even when they currently hold a

competitive advantage in the market. Competition is

aggressively seeking new resources and capabilities for value

creation for both customer and shareholders. Therefore

businesses are constantly endeavoring to identify, create, and

implement strategies to achieve competitive advantage from

which they establish superior profitability and revenue growth.

Sustaining requires plans that go beyond the incremental

improvements associated with operations excellence tools.

Creation and sustainment requires breakthrough elements which transform an organization into something better – something different.

There are two aspects associated with sustaining competitive advantage from operations excellence. First, many businesses seek to implement strategies leading to a competitive advantage. Many of these strive through some course of time to introduce new products and services, or to implement a process improvement that establishes a cost reduction in the business structure. Nevertheless, competitors are fast to emulate these new services, products, or reduce cost structures. Therefore, the competitive gain is short lived since it is reproducible by others in the market.

The second aspect, the key to implementation of operations excellence with sustainment, is a developmental plan that creates the organizational culture that permeates the business. When lean manufacturing techniques are grounded in the culture they become the very business system. As the operations excellence culture develops a level of maturity the organizations resource capabilities form distinctive competencies. These resources are focused and aligned so that new values, expectations, and behaviors fully support the strategy through adaptation and learning.

Yet, according to industry surveys nearly two thirds of the companies implementing operations excellence fail in the endeavor after many months of efforts and sizeable expenditures. The difference lies in the fact that when a company's strategy changes in a major way, the culture must breakthrough as well to support the new strategy. What separates the successful company from the attempts that fail?

With the extensive focus on lean manufacturing throughout industry, nearly all management members have heard of the terms or have some level of familiarity with the techniques; recognizing that if successful these techniques lead to major improvements in decreased quality issues, decreased lead time to the customers, and reduced cost structures. In the rush to implement, many companies identified target areas within the organizations that obviously required improvement, most commonly the areas associated directly with manufacturing are selected. Then rapidly announce and initiate their operations excellence programs with the idea that they will attain high impact results with intent to emulate the premier benchmark in manufacturing operations, Toyota and the TPS.

Toyota's manufacturing plant in Georgetown, KY opens its doors to plant tours attended by seekers of the key to operations excellence. The attendees on many tours include direct competitors of Toyota. The tour participants ask questions concerning Kanban, SMED, TPM activities etc. throughout the tour while the host graciously provides detailed information on the topics. Many participants return to their businesses and attempt to emulate Toyota by copying the techniques that were demonstrated. Most are unsuccessful in the endeavor to improved results simply because they failed to notice, appreciate, and develop the understanding of Toyota's underlying culture that drives its success – the true distinctive competency that is not easily copied and therefore the sustainable competitive advantage.

Toyota and the few other world class businesses who have matured an excellence in operations confound the seekers with their competitive advantage. Each year the market is blasted with a seamlessly ending list of new books, seminars, and consultants that only reinforce the thoughts that the techniques of lean manufacturing are the right choices to achieve economic success. Yet, these endless lines of experts and advice fail to provide the important key of operations excellence – how.

Businesses armed with world class benchmarks, books, consultants, and desires to execute their new strategy launch their initiative. A champion is appointed as a program manager for lean, then the management teams steps back and await updates on progress as well as the performance improvements gained. It is typical to see activities deployed throughout the manufacturing locations in small pilot areas with such elements as Kanban, TPM, SMED, and Continuous Flow. Many of these attempts are through the efforts of teams formed and structured for one time kaizen events specifically aimed to fix an issue or gain rapid results. Many events manage to gain some level of improvement with the initial efforts, however, when followed up in several weeks or months the performance levels have decreased with results returning to previous metric levels.

These traditional approaches of implementation are associated with incremental change, single one time events, piecemeal and haphazard execution with no follow up accountability. Little or no change leadership effort is put forth to develop understanding of why the change is needed, nor create a sense of urgency in all employees in a fashion that outlines what the changes mean to "me", how these changes effect my job, my role, and how I will fit into the changed organization.

This traditional, result based implementation model does not seek to establish an overall vision of what the operation will look like in the future and how kaizen events fit into the creation of that vision. Leadership in many cases fail to engage themselves and set the example while building commitment in the teams, many times only inquiring once per month as to the results gained with their attention drawn to poor performance and viewed as a punitive follow up. The workforce sees little on the floor application of change leadership by example and daily involvement.

Further complicating the traditional approach, leadership fails to align and integrate the entire organization including the support functions. This lack of cross functional ownership permits current methods such as performance evaluations, reward system, job classifications, and overall metrics to remain in place. Status quo in support areas coupled with emphasis on old performance standards and behaviors sends a mixed message to all employees that the change is localized versus system wide.

To create an environment that can sustain improvements, the business must establish breakthroughs in resource capabilities that mature into distinctive competencies. These distinctive competencies are unique strengths within the organization resources enabling the company to achieve a lower cost structure or differentiate its products and services from the competition. These capabilities are gained through creation of an organizational culture that fosters learning and experimentation to improve. A culture supported by new values, expectations, behaviors, organizational structure alignment and integration, as well as the improvement of processes throughout the operation, all accomplished in a supportive way that enables strategic intent. These intangible capabilities; resources that are capable, flexible and reliable are the essence of sustainable competitive advantage through operations excellence.

Sustainable competitive advantage is gained through development and maturity of resource capabilities that transform the culture; intangible capabilities that are not reproducible by others in the marketplace. Resources are physical and non-physical elements within the organization such as equipment, technology, employees, capital, culture, etc. that allow the business to create value for a customer. More importantly, capability refers to a company's skill at coordinating and utilization of resources effectively. A major distinction in business is that a company may have unlimited resources yet lack capabilities to utilize these assets effectively and efficiently, thereby having no distinctive competencies.

This traditional model of deployment is reinforced through examination of corporate operations excellence and Lean Enterprise Manuals for several Fortune 500 companies clearly highlighting the depth of strategic intent, understanding, and approach to operations excellence. Each examination found volumes of information detailing the very specific aspects of lean manufacturing techniques. However, none of the manuals included information concerning change leadership, organizational culture, or basic leadership content; how to transform the organization.

As a vital as operations excellence strategic initiatives are for increased competitive advantage, companies repeatedly fail to gain anticipated results or to complete the implementation as originated. Current models have common barriers to their success which must be recognized, understood, and dealt with by leadership. These barriers include;

- Lack of focus
- No compelling reason to change
- Sponsorship is lacking
- Rush to implement with out development
- Misalignment
- Low commitment
- No follow through discipline
- Little or no communication
- Lack of leadership by example

The real and lasting successful implementations are achieved through creating the right balance between incremental improvements and breakthrough change that make lasting modification within the organizations culture. As Tom Peters (1997) writes in *The Circle of Innovation:*

If you're spending every waking professional hour making "it" a bit better today than yesterday, then...necessarily...you aren't spending every waking hour working on reinventing it, blowing it up. The two notions are in tension. The two are opposites. The mindset and emotional bent of "a little bit better" is not less than antithetical to the mindset and emotional bent of "re-invent it"/"blow it up. (p. 27)

Every functional area, each level of the organization must be

Involved and requires engagement, entire organizational structures, processes, and control systems must be re-established to support and sustain the competitive advantage sought. Organizations are a linkage of systems and relationships, and changing one area often creates necessary changes in other areas. When deploying lean manufacturing, the development must include changes in the total operation.

This study will examine the importance of change leadership in operations excellence transformation and create understanding of the specific roles leadership must accomplish through developmental phases to ensure success through removal of the barriers. Change leadership in essence must create the organizations new structures, processes, and control systems that support a culture of operations excellence. Research within this study will focus on the identification of key change leadership elements essential to success and the creation of a new developmental model for operations excellence transformation. The study will be broken into three phases of which the first phase will seek to identify barriers to successful implementation in comparison of traditional models to models built upon change.

An operations excellence initiative is truly one of change versus simply the narrow implementation of lean manufacturing techniques in some location of the operation. To achieve operations excellence the business will need to transform the organization into something better, something different. Leadership of cultural change becomes as vital to the transformation as the specific techniques themselves. Leadership must address each of the factors associated with failure and ensure that the new structures, processes, and control systems exemplifies expectations of the new desired performance behaviors and values through focus and alignment of the total organization.

Secondly, surveys will be utilized to identify current business strategies and prioritization levels being given by companies. This will include surveys to establish the level of achievement as well as determination of barriers that impede successful deployment. The intent is to compile a listing of the elements that create implementation issues and barriers. A final set of surveys will use fifteen questions focused upon change leadership and organizational transformation being sent to two groups of business members. The first study group will be senior management teams within business ranging from CEO to Plant Manager level participants. The counter part survey will be sent to mid level management members through operators at the lower levels of the structure. The study will look for any gap in the perceived level of successful achievement of the individual elements in question. This will provide identification of any differentiation between organizational levels and the successful roll out of implementation of change.

The conclusion of the study will lead to a proposed new fully integrated model for operations excellence transformation. This model will combine the existing model of lean manufacturing techniques with the key change leadership elements identified from the surveys. Any additional

recommendations will be identified for further study.

CHAPTER 2: REVIEW OF RELATED LITERATURE

Introduction

The journey to operations excellence is one of various change actions and techniques focused to deliver superior performance in efficiency, quality, innovation, and customer responsiveness. This journey entails much more than the completion of certain techniques of lean manufacturing; it is profoundly about organizational transformation. To succeed in the strategic intent of operations excellence the overall organization must be ready and willing to drive change to every function of the structure, processes, and culture. Moreover, to succeed to a level where operations excellence becomes a sustainable competitive advantage, the organization must be transformed into something better, something different. Gordon Sullivan and Michael V. Harper (1996) in *Hope is Not a Method: What Business Leaders Can Learn from America's Army,* define:

The intent of transformation is not simply to accommodate discontinuities or to "keep up" with changes in process or changes benchmarked by others; it is, rather, to move into the future and create a new standard.

(p. 157)

History is full of businesses that over time lost competitive position and in many cases became complacent within the market. New global competition through innovative start up companies and low cost producers leave these businesses in a position where simple survival becomes the basic drive both strategically and tactically. As Gary Hamel and C.K. Prahalad (1994) point out in, *Competing for the Future: Breakthrough Strategies for Seizing Control of Your Industry and Creating the Markets of Tomorrow:*

> These and many other companies found themselves confronted with sizable "organizational transformation" problems. Of course, any company that is more of a bystander than a driver on the road to the future will find its structure, values, and skills becoming progressively less attuned to an ever-changing industry reality. Such a discrepancy between the pace of

change in the industry environment and the pace of change in the internal environment spawns the daunting tasks of organizational transformation. (p. 6)

The old principles of traditional business no longer work. The fundamental shift in global complexity and chaotic transition requires operations excellence transformation on an unprecedented scale. The new models for business will still be built upon the basic elements of vision, strategy, objectives and goals but add the vital aspects of organizational development and cultural transformation founded on new expectations, development, and capabilities of internal resources. To achieve sustainable competitive advantage, a new business model based on the same building blocks of the traditional corporation must emerge to include the change leadership aspects of; learning, focus, alignment, and sustainment. As Michael Cowley and Ellen Domb (1997) explain in, *Beyond Strategic Vision: Effective Corporate Action with Hoshin Planning,* "genuine learning is the process of generating new capability or capacity in the organization" (p.131).

In the past, strategic business models have typically focused upon external factors of competitiveness. Internal to the organization, management would call upon cost containment and reduction to offset the less than stellar sales numbers. In the rush to gain rapid improvement in the company value to the shareholders, cost reduction efforts took on many names such as re-engineering, downsizing, right-sizing, and in many cases lean manufacturing. But in reality, these programs become reduction in workforce numbers, overhead, and rationalization of business operations efforts including layoffs and plant closures; commonly referred to more often as *mean manufacturing*.

> In a world where competitors are capable of achieving 5, 10, or 15% real growth in revenues, aggressive denominator reduction, under a flat revenue stream, is simply a way to sell market share profitability. Marketing strategists term this a "harvest strategy" and consider it a no-brainer. (Hamel and Prahalad, 1994, p. 9)

These companies sacrificed their future competitiveness in lieu of rapid bottom line results. Competing for tomorrow and beyond involves operations excellence built upon resource capabilities and process improvements that establish distinctive competencies within the organization not mere headcount reductions or one time change events. When such a business initiative as operations excellence is launched, management must clearly understand that for the creation of sustainable competitive advantage the organization must go beyond the mere conducting of a kaizen events focused upon specific techniques such as SMED or Kanban, etc. These various techniques of lean manufacturing are simply that, techniques that can be reproduced by any business and hence not a competitive advantage. John Allen, Charles Robinson, and Dave Stewart (2001) in *Lean Manufacturing: A Plant Floor Guide,* state:

> Awareness of and attention to change management principles and the dynamics of change are necessary for a successful transition to a lean environment. When changes are made to an operation, project mangers and lean implementers must be sensitive to change issues because most employees have not worked in a lean

environment. Also, behavioral changes are required as lean plants set different expectations for performance and emphasize values different from traditional manufacturing. What worked in the old system probably will not work in the lean production system. (p.157)

Fundamentally, operations excellence is more about organizational culture change than the techniques of lean manufacturing. Hence, vital to the sustainability of the results gained is the transformation of the organization culture as William M. Feld (2001) comments in *Lean Manufacturing: Tools, Techniques, and How to Use Them:*

> True competitive advantage comes from instilling capability within the workforce, and this can only be accomplished through: (1) achieving demonstrated knowledge transfer by building an empowered workforce, (2) engaging all employees within the business by steering their collective energies in the same direction, and (3) empowering the workforce with

clarified expectations, common purpose, and accountability to get the job done. (p. 6)

Typically, businesses approach operations excellence as a series of single events highly in a specific area. This approach of incremental change through a progression of events maintains the organizations status quo with only limited impact in a targeted area. Incremental change then occurs through unchanged structure, process, and controls. Whereas, to achieve operations excellence that is sustainable requires transformation through radical change; change that breaks the status quo by transforming the total organization with breakthrough in the creation of new structures, processes and culture that enable the strategic intent.

Successful sustainable execution must have its roots in the empowerment and engagement of all employees through actionable items for which they have control, ownership, and ability to influence. This ground level focus upon actionable items allows the improvements to take place at the level of impact by individuals who know the details and own the items thereby creating the sustainable shift in expectations, behavior and culture; non-reproducible competencies that provide competitive advantage.

Strategic realization of operations excellence must therefore include in its model all the aspects of change leadership and organizational culture. As Willie Pietersen (2002) points out in, *Reinventing Strategy: Using Strategic Learning to Create & Sustain Breakthrough Performance:* "the central challenge facing managers today is to create and lead an adaptive enterprise – an organization with the built-in ability to sense and rapidly adjust to change on a continuous basis" (p.2). Pietersen goes on to write that:

> Sustainable competitive advantage cannot come from any particular product or service, no matter how good it may be. Those things have a short shelf life. In today's marketplace it is the organizational capability to adapt that is the only sustainable competitive advantage. (p.2)

Thus, sustainable competitive advantage can only be achieved based upon a solid foundation of operations excellence culture.

Traditional Operations Excellence Business Models

To remain competitive in the market requires management to take an active role in recognizing and acknowledging that the business environment is changing daily. As Sullivan and Harper (1996) explain, "today, we face fundamental shifts in technology, markets, human resource development, global distribution, information management, government intervention, and other critical dimensions of the strategic environments in which we operate" (p.152). Time and distance have been compressed to a point that their presence only ensures that somewhere a business interest is in progress or about to launch that can provide the same product or services faster, cheaper, and with better quality.

Every business concern must clearly understand that "competitors appear without warning to thunder against their market share in yet another full frontal no-holds barred assault. Under constant attack, the traditional businesses are falling back in marker after market" (Lareau, 2000, p.2). The consumer's dollar is global in reach to a market with capacity built on start up companies and emerging countries that establish a capability to meet and exceed what were once thought of unbeatable companies in market share position.

The challenge for business is more than simple survival but how to keep a step ahead of the competition. Success in business doesn't come from feeling comfortable, business life cycles have accelerated to a pace requiring operational excellence through transformation of the complete organization. Recent decades have witnessed dramatic changes shaping the economy and business environment which has radically altered the requirements for building and managing a successful business. If a business is going to withstand relentless and constantly growing global competition, it must radically change its ways of doing business requiring a fundamental shift in the organization culture.

Traditional strategy models, such as Michael Porter's Five Forces, concentrate on the company's external competitive environment. Therefore, most organizations fail to look inside the company while conducting strategic planning sessions which is defined by Cowley and Domb (1997) as "to set the direction of the organization to improve its prospects for long-term survival and prosperity" (p. 3).

Typical to Porter's model, management details a listing of strategic objectives for business growth, product development, market penetration, customer service, and increase in profitability. In most cases the annual analysis relies heavily upon external conditions to the business, such as how to acquire business through new product development or acquisition, global markets, customer service levels, social, technical and political aspects impacting the business. Since growing the business, launching new products or penetrating a new market are more difficult than slashing cost, the primary go to plan in traditional organizations typically will include some aspect of operations excellence as back up to ensure return on investment and shareholder value.

What occurs is more operational planning than strategic planning and a one time event rather than an ongoing process. The plan becomes a wish list of non-integrated actions that are tactical in nature to ensure rapid results and include no major operations excellence breakthrough initiatives failing to elevate the organization to support the strategic intent of competitive advantage. The senior management team has developed a list of action steps versus creative new concepts or breakthroughs of true strategy which Pietersen (2002) defines as:

> Strategy determines how you will use your scarce resources in the best way possible. If resources were unlimited, then there would be no need for strategy; we could survive indefinitely by throwing time and money and people at out problems until our obstacles and competitors were simply overwhelmed. (p.41)

From initial inception, the strategic objectives of operations excellence become the drivers of improvements in productivity and profitability through current in vogue techniques such as lean manufacturing. In the traditionally modeled organization initiatives are taken entirely upon what can be implemented to improve a process and show performance results that impact the bottom line fast. The operations excellence strategic plan is interpreted by management as a set of independent tactical actions and goals rather than breakthrough transformations. As the strategic plan is handed down, each organizational level takes a narrow minded view based upon past history of such initiatives that the mandate is to gain profitability and productivity through cost reductions.

Many times these objectives and goals are set arbitrarily by each prior level of management without development of an understanding of the competitive requirements, urgency of the need for change, or a clear view of the organization as a total integrated system. Allen et al. (2001) explain:

> Traditionally, companies have always had some form of policy deployment. However, polices are often created by high-level managers and mandated to the rest of the company, without sufficient empowerment or resources given to employees to accomplish the desired results. These business plans typically are disconnected from the rest of the organization, and there is little involvement from those who have the most influence on achieving the business plan – the workers. (p.220)

Organizations designed for industrial age competition have central control and large functional departments. Strategy is developed at the top and implemented downward through the central command and control culture. Change occurs rarely and as such is implemented incrementally allowing management time for slow reaction and control via budgets. Such methods are inadequate in rapidly changing environments creating difficulty in implementation of breakthrough initiatives and transformation; hierarchy protects the two enemies of change, bureaucracy and compliancy.

Unfortunately, hierarchical companies are better at telling people what to do than at getting employees to collaborate. When hierarchy dominates the culture, corporate managers do all the thinking, control access to information, and tell everyone what to do. Effective change demands collaboration between willing and motivated individuals, under these circumstances collaboration is an unnatural act. This command and control structure only works well when the edict is to reduce cost and gain improved bottom line results rapidly.

Year after year business organizations go through the motions with hierarchical structure of command and control functionality that serves to dilute the strategic process into a cost reduction knee jerk. The lack of a strategic process frequently results in objectives and goals that are very broad in scope and set blindly to the operation with what Pietersen (2002) describes, "very little evidence of creative, long term thinking about changes in the competitive environment and how the company must deploy its scarce resources in response to those changes" (p.44).

With such a wide scope approach to operations excellence the push for internal cost reductions creates an abundance of opportunities for which Hamel and Prahalad (1994) reaffirm that "...many firms, finding themselves behind on cost, quality, cycle time, customer service and other parameters, attempt to put everything right simultaneously, and then wonder why progress is so painfully slow" (p.162). It is a natural tendency for management to over commit the organization leading to little progress and high stress levels. Frustration builds from executives down through the management ranks as results are not gained or take longer than expected. "Without focused attention on a few key operational goals at any one time, improvement efforts are likely to be so diluted that the firm ends up as a perpetual laggard in every critical performance area" (Hamel & Prahalad, 1994, p.162).

Since the overall plan fails to identify the few critical objectives and initiatives that all functions within the organization should align to, many operations turn strictly to a manufacturing and production perspective, not as an organization wide endeavor requiring integration and alignment of all functions from a total systems point of view. Hamel and Prahalad (1994) site the example,

> Although GM was powerful in terms of resources, its lack of a unifying sense of purpose meant that individual efforts were likely to be cumulative. A lack of direction almost ensure that units will work at cross-purposes, that priorities will be set capriciously, and that consistency will too often be sacrificed on the altar of expediency (p.130).

Total business organization engagement is lacking for cross functional ownership and overall business systems integration to support the desired expectations in performance.

Examples abound, such as the production department implementing a new kanban method to replenish material at the assembly line reducing both time and amount of inventory held on hand. However, the materials department having not been assigned any ownership nor commitment to the change fails to develop a process which coordinates this new lean materials process in the plant with external suppliers who continue to ship large quantities of parts only to be stored in another location of the plant. Inventory reduction did not occur, the inventory was simply shifted to another location due to lack of alignment between the internal functions. This misalignment of resources and actions stems from the lack of understanding of the strategy intent coupled with vision of the organization in the future. Kaplan and Norton (2001) explain that:

> In this era of knowledge workers, strategy must be executed at all levels of the organization. People must change their behaviors and adopt new values. The key to this transformation is putting strategy at the center of the management process. Strategy cannot be executed if it cannot be understood, however, and it cannot be understood if it cannot be described. (pp. 65-66)

Frequently the failure to align to the few critical objectives and integrate the entire organization into a focused operations excellence model can be found in polices and procedures. Lean manufacturing is launched within areas of the operation with expressed desires of improved performance and concepts such as teamwork. Yet, performance metrics and reviews are not changed to support the new strategy. Old polices and procedures continue to reinforce the old behaviors and values, leading to a lack of improvement. Pietersen (2002) writes:

> Whenever you measure an activity within your company, you are inevitably doing two things: You are gauging its performance, and you are sending the message, "This is important."...You cannot hope to achieve your new strategy if you continue to measure and reward the old one.

> (p.65)

Examples of traditional misalignment include a materials' function assigning a process change and metric to the receiving department that tracks inventory dollar value remaining on the incoming dock each day. The receiving department management determines that in order to achieve the daily target metric, that excessive and/or old inventory will be moved to other locations in the operation to simply show low dollar value in receiving. No true process change or cost reductions have occurred, yet management reports that the department is meeting its assigned target. Further examples include the individual performance reviews based upon traditional criteria of management style that promotes and encourages individual performance above team based concepts coupled with tactical daily management versus breakthrough strategic efforts. The individual who hordes knowledge and is the fire fighting crisis fixer remains looked upon as a hero and during reviews is rewarded based on outmoded policies and procedures.

The lack of focus and alignment of actions with sponsors and owners creates an ad hoc approach to execution that is easily diverted from the true strategic intent by tactical actions not directly supporting the strategy. As such, strategy falls to the wayside in lieu of day to day crisis management. Pietersen (2002) sites a classic study by Henry Mintzberg pointing out that:

Fully 90 percent of the results projected in most companies' formal strategic planning processes never come to fruition...Only 10 percent of most companies' actions arise out of their strategic planning ("realized strategy"). But what is the source of the other 90 percent of what companies do? Mintzberg calls it "emergent strategy." This describes the series of ad-hoc initiatives, reactions, decisions, and choices that managers make in response to daily pressures, without guidance from any overarching strategic concept. Taken together, they amount to the real strategy that most companies follow. (pp.44 - 45)

Characteristically, the action items are viewed from a technical stand point relying upon new equipment, automated processes, as well as management programs such as *Total Quality Management* (TQM), *Management By Objectives* (MBO), *Re-Engineering* and current approaches such as lean manufacturing. Each of these programs throughout business history have been added to as Lareau (2000) declares a "list of all the fads and gimmicks that have been dragged through training rooms and business magazines over the past 50 years...They were usually just tools and approaches or concepts that addressed only one particular aspect of a business" (p.18).

Many operations excellence efforts specifically focus upon the maximized utilization of equipment and technology. Many include the launch of the endeavor with the acquisition of new capital equipment employing new technology and greater levels of capacity for production. The focus has always lacked workforce and human development, the key aspect of knowledge. This area of resource management is vital since many companies have the capital to throw resources at an issue to increase capacity or provide needed focus; however, simply throwing bodies at an issue only provides short lived increases without sustainability.

A firm can sit atop mountains of cash and command legions of talented people, and still lose its preeminent position.... The point here is that too often competitors are judged in terms of resources rather than resourcefulness....Resourcefulness stems not from an elegantly structured strategic architecture, but from a deeply felt sense of purpose, a broadly shared dream, a truly seductive view of tomorrow's opportunities. (Hamel & Prahalad, 1994, p.128)

This linkage to technical management stems from classic business theory for management which reflects three vital areas of skill for managers; conceptual, people, and technical. Traditional management has a tendency to provide solutions founded only on technical and conceptual, ignoring the people aspect. Even though people skills are vital at all levels of the hierarchy for managers this is the area that over the years has had the least attention within business schools and organizations as a whole. Many executives leading transformational change are comfortable dealing with 'hard' managerial and technical issues but reluctant to tackle the 'soft' human resource aspects of radical change. Yet the broad scope of the change, the accelerated pace, and the desire for an order of magnitude improvement in performance have such dramatic implications for individual employees throughout the whole organization that dealing with human resource issues is of crucial importance to the ultimate success of the change effort.

Prior to any change, job definitions, tasks, responsibilities and boundaries to neighboring functions may be relatively clear. During the course of the change process, however, many of these may become blurred as people are required to take on greater responsibility, wonder why the change is occurring, and concerned how the change will affect them via new or revised expectations. All this can cause anxiety, fear, reluctance or even rejection of the change because it is not at all clear to people what their status, role, responsibility, competency, span of authority and relationship to bosses, peers and staff will be in the future, the very things by which people tend to define themselves. The feelings are quite different from the way in which they have been traditionally viewed yet the very reason the deployment of operations excellence must be transformational to impact fundamental changes in the organizational culture.

Approaching operations excellence as a back up strategy for cost reductions coupled with unrealistic expectations in the time frame for results only highlights the lack of understanding by management that to achieve operations excellence competitive advantage that is sustainable will encompass transforming the organizational culture; the expectations, values, and norms. Allen et al. (2001) declare that criteria for success as, "behavioral changes are required as lean plants set different expectations for performance and emphasize values different from traditional manufacturing. What worked in the old system probably will not work in the lean production system" (p.157).

The decade of the nineties was full of cost reduction programs such as downsizing, rationalization, right sizing and re-engineering; programs that without preparation work up front by management to create vision, strategic intent, and change leadership, only become buzzwords with no substance. The up front work is essential to the overall transformation and when missing, the strategy simply becomes the flavor of the day. Sullivan and Harper (1996) express this important concept as:

Simply improving an existing process will not solve a problem. This is the failure of the "R-words" – reshaping, reengineering, reinventing, and reposturing. *Doing the same thing you have always done – no matter how much you improve it - will get you only what you had before.* The old ways lead to the same old failures. (p.152)

True to traditional models, operations excellence has been caught up in the train of taught singularly focused on rapid cost reduction. The emergence and utilization of management fads corresponds to the strategic uncertainty within businesses that have become a substitute for real strategy. Lareau (2000) is quick to point out:

> The right sizing frenzy has been so wholeheartedly embraced that it has begun to assume the appearance of a business strategy...But rightsizing and cost cutting is not a strategy. It is a knee jerk reflex to financial parameters and short term profit pressure from company boards and stockholders. Rightsizing only accomplishes one thing; it reduces cost in the short term. (p. 20)

Programs such as right sizing and reengineering simply miss the world class challenge of people and organization culture. Very few executives and businesses turn to the development and creation of resource capabilities in traditional model companies. In fact, the application of rightsizing, re-engineering, etc. is counter to the development of the workforce by reducing headcount and thereby removing skills and knowledge from the organization. This leaves less resources to accomplish necessary activities, creates loss of knowledge, builds fear and stress in the overworked employees that remain and fosters feelings of disloyalty to the organization in the realization that they may be the next to go. Lareau (2000) writes that, "a traditional organization routinely and deliberately compromises human dignity and need satisfaction for no other purpose than to maintain the caste system and the authority of the management structure" (p.81).

Traditional managers are trained for and promoted by results; they have come to view the techniques of operations excellence as the hard stuff and not to be concerned with people skills or the soft stuff (Figure 2). To reinforce this conditioned training, multitudes of books, seminars, articles, and consulting gurus have specialized in operations excellence; lean manufacturing techniques. Any books store will have copies of the latest techniques and applications for the hard stuff associated with lean manufacturing while consultants are ready to extol the benefits by spending numerous resources, time, and cash to pursuit of a model that relies upon implementation of technical solutions such as Kanban, SMED, JIT or TPM.

Whether in a book, a seminar, or by a consultant, the failure in this traditional model is that of implementation road maps that are full of "what to do" without providing understanding of the importance of organizational dynamics, culture, individual and group behaviors; the "how", as a supporting foundation to the technical skills required to create true competencies within resources. Feld (2002) writes that:

> When initiatives focus on just the mechanics and techniques, the improvement is more about calculations and formulas than it is about improving workforce capability. Anyone can read a book, run a numbers analysis on demand behavior, calculate takt time, and establish a U-shaped layout, but doing so is not what will make a company differ from its competition. (p.5)

One of the leading experts of lean manufacturing, James Womack typifies this traditional scenario with several best selling books that provide page upon page of theories while outlining the benefits of why lean should be accomplished at any business. Nevertheless, he fails to provide the "how", the practical understanding of how operations excellence should be developed and implemented through transforming the organization culture for sustainable competitive advantage, not just the one time events that can be rapidly reproduced by any other company.

The hard stuff, technical tools and techniques are actions that can be reproduced by the competition and hence do not provide a sustainable competitive advantage. Whereas, focus upon the development of resource capabilities transforms the organization; "It is not cash that fuels the journey to the future, but the emotional and intellectual energy of every employee" (Hamel & Prahalad, 1994, p. 127). Development of resources and cultural capabilities establishes a distinctive competency which can not be reproduced by the competition therefore leading to a sustainable competitive advantage.

Traditional conditions of poor strategic planning as outlined above are coupled with a lack of a vision that is shared throughout the total organization. Senior level managers may have a vision of the business future, but no one else does. This tends to lead to a workforce that is uninspired with non-coordinated efforts, many functionally opposed to the overall strategic desire. Without a shared vision there is no understanding of why the strategic initiative of operations excellence must be successfully implemented. Lareau (2000) cites:

> Unfortunately, for many companies, having well-defined vision statements changes nothing within the organization. The exercise of creating a vision becomes a waste of time and talent when the statement is used for nothing more than being published in the annual report or being displayed in a reception area or printed on wallet cards. (p.166)

Lareau goes on to point out the importance of vision citing "Dr. Deming's first point: 'Achieve constancy of purpose'" (p. 166).

Many businesses, in effort to gain buy in to the strategic intent and vision, go to the extent of announcing the initiative through mass briefings or the fanfare of t-shirts, banners, coffee mugs, etc. Nevertheless, there is little or no communications as to why the initiative is required, what the initiative will include, or how this will impact the individual employees on a, what does this me to me level. This lack of communication is further complicated by management not establishing a sense of urgency as to why the change is necessary. As Kaplan and Norton (2001) describe "strategy cannot be executed if it cannot be understood, however, and it cannot be understood if it cannot be described" (pp. 65-66).

Lack of communications fosters an environment in which the entire workforce including management labor under the impression that the business is doing well enough, products and services meet customer demand, and competitively the market is remaining status quo. Information such as operations performance is not track or talked about at important levels of the organization, middle management down to the workforce. The traditional model protects the command and control structure so that only the upper levels of management know what is happening in the business and market place. Yet, it is typical that within the upper ranks there is little understanding of the business position, competitive issues, or consensus as to what initiatives to prioritize and a narrowly focused view based on functional aspects versus system wide integration. Typically, this silo approach tends to develop the view that my department is doing well; it's the others that need to change or improve. Overall, no change occurs and compliancy takes hold.

Management must understand that to remain idle, complacent, or willing to endure in status quo only means death to a business in today's market. Lareau (2000) declares:

> Nothing is static in an organization. Even when it seems as if nothing is happening, an organization is calcifying and sedimentizing towards traditional norms, no matter where it started. The first and foremost function of enlightened leaders is to actively challenge this evolution every second. (p.78)

Leaders of companies must not fall into common complacency traps (Figure 3) such as doing things too well, being in the wrong business, or making yesterday perfect. Allen et al. (2001) have defined compliancy as, "the status quo is the comfort zone in most traditional manufacturing environments. Doing things as they have always been done is more important than innovation or change" (p.168).

Doing things too well is common in businesses that have or are currently succeeding in markets and business performance. Management fails to recognize the dynamics of change in global industry and tend to rest on their laurels of past success. They lose touch with the real conditions and strategic environment of customers, competition, and internal performance only to remain successful for short period of time then one day find that their market share has decreased and productivity lagging to the point they no longer maintain profitability. "A laggard is a company where senior managers believe they know more about how the industry works than they actually do, and where what they do know is out of date" (Hamel and Prahalad, 1994, p.55).

The complacency of being in the wrong business again points to a management team that has failed to pay close attention to global markets and customer demands only to provide out dated products or services. Finally, the complacency of making yesterday perfect, finds a management team that is working diligently to improve process and capabilities, but based on past structures, processes, and control methods leading to hard work but no successful change in business performance or value creation to customers and shareholders. John Kotter (1996) in Leading Change states "a good rule of thumb in a major change effort is: Never underestimate the magnitude of the forces that reinforce complacency and that help maintain the status quo" (p.42).

The inertia associated with compliancy is the first major hurdle and critical step for management in the business to overcome when moving to implement operations excellence. Management must develop the clear understanding of how the global market is changing, how new competitive factors are being created and how those factors impact their business. "What prevents companies from creating the future is an installed base of thinking the unquestioned conventions, the myopic view of opportunities and threats, and the unchallenged precedents that comprise the existing managerial frame" (Hamel and Pahalad,1994, p.61).

Internally, management must recognize that past success does not ensure future success and that the performance of resources and capabilities must be constantly reviewed and set to newer, higher levels of expectations to focus and drive internal improvement. Furthermore, the hard work of management must set a tempo of urgency that overcomes the status quo. Sullivan and Harper (1996) assert that:

> Leading change means doing two jobs at once – getting the organization through today and getting the organization into tomorrow. Most people will be slow to understand the need for change, preferring the future to look like today, thus displacing their lives and sense of reality as little as possible. Transformational leadership requires a personal and very hands-on approach, taking and directing action, building the confidence necessary for people to let go of today's paradigm and move into the future. (p. 236)

Traditionally, during execution of action events the status of the operations excellence plan is not frequently or carefully reviewed on an ongoing basis which tends to create the impression that the plans are not taken seriously by management. Management is seen by the entire workforce as not engaged, stepping up to committed interest or following through with any level of feedback. In the day to day firefighting and functional silos management has no time to gather as a team to provide guidance, prioritization of actions, or constructive feedback.

Since progress is not monitored, utilization of resources not confirmed, controlled or coordinated, and results not verified to overall performance objectives, the workforce perceives a lack on interest in the strategic endeavor. In traditional command and control the process of follow up typically draws attention only when desired results and cost reductions are not achieved and therefore punitive versus constructive feedback promoting experimentation and learning. This method only serves to create fear and an environment that disguises true results while constraining the ability for creative thinking and learning that is required for breakthrough initiatives.

For most traditional businesses, the command and control process is built around a monthly operating budget control meeting devoted to review of performance versus budget, why the variances occurred, and what countermeasure are necessary next month to get back on target. This small showing of dedication to review is reactive based versus forward looking strategically for breakthroughs. Kaplan and Norton (2001) point out that, "our research indicates that 85 percent of management teams spend less than one hour per month discussing strategy" (p.14).

Based on the low success rates of establishing a competitive advantage through operations excellence based on traditional models of incremental change and limited scope miss the two outcomes provided by transformation; breakthrough and continuous change. Results can be rapidly gained through single event implementation of techniques but overall success rates resulting from sustainment are minimal. To achieve the sustainable competitive advantage looked for there must be a radical change consisting of breakthroughs as well as continuous improvement to effect total organizational structures, processes and controls thereby creating a new culture. A culture based on operations excellence that has built distinctive competencies based on resource capabilities.

In the single event frame of mind, management assigns a SMED event to a particular machine in hopes that reduced set up time will increase productivity and hence greater capacity with higher profitability. This incremental change is conducted through the application of the techniques of SMED with little training and lack of communications to the operators as to why the change is necessary, how it impacts their daily job, and more importantly seeking input from them as process owners as to what could be changed to reduce set up times.

Instead of utilizing the operators' expertise, management ignores their input and alienates their buy in by mandating changes that operators had no part of creating. Nevertheless, some results are gained but once the project manager leaves the area, old behaviors and methods will return to pre-event norms. The traditional model creates no sustainable change in culture, incremental gains were established briefly but without transforming the organization as a total system change to support performance gains are unsustained. A prime example of the traditional view of competitive advantage of operations excellence and management's fascination with fast results lead many to benchmark themselves to Toyota and the TPS.

At its manufacturing facility near Lexington, Kentucky Toyota opens its doors to plant tours by numerous groups including management members from various industries including direct competitors. These groups tour the operation and are encouraged to ask questions at the end of the tour concerning what was viewed as best practices or of particular interest. Nonetheless, the questions largely fall to how do specific techniques such as kanban get developed and implemented from a technical aspect. Rarely does a participant ask the Toyota team how they lead organizational transformation or how operations excellence was developed to a level that it provides a culture of continuous improvement.

Toyota leads the market in various aspects and recently has moved into a position replacing a top three original American automotive manufacturer. So far, Toyota has no fear of conducting these tours and openly invites and encourages these. Why? Toyota's operation excellence is founded in its culture, the very values, expectations and behaviors of every employee supported by organizational structures, processes and controls that sustains their competitive advantage. Toyota recognizes that the capability, flexibility and reliability of its resources are the foundation of distinctive competencies that others have difficulty reproducing. Distinctive competencies that go well beyond the single event application of techniques of lean manufacturing that can be reproduced by any business and hence lead to Toyota's sustainable competitive advantage.

Businesses have reached the limits of the traditional model's effectiveness with respect to staying ahead of complexity and speed of change creating a mismatch between today's competitive environment and the classic business model. Lareau (2000) declares that up till now, "most organizations fail to achieve world-class status simply because they are traditional organizations rather than because of bad decisions. Traditional organizations make bad decisions for the same reason that water is wet; it is their nature" (p.78). Traditional management has followed an outdated business model that has focused upon external development with little or no concern for long term creation of value internally to the organization. Sustainable competitive advantage must be founded upon resources that are capable, flexible, and reliable in operations excellence hence the establishment of distinctive competencies.

Management has missed the opportunity to create this transformation to operations excellence with the failure to build an understanding and urgency as to why change is necessary, a vision as to what the future condition of the organization will look like, lack of communication of the vision, and why and how it affects each individual.

In the rush to achieve rapid high impact results management forgoes the time to establish a detailed plan for implementation of operations excellence in lieu of one time technical fixes. Finally, management fails to consider the long term development of resource capabilities through creation of breakthrough transformation in culture coupled with continuous improvement. Lareau (2000) writes, "the reasons why most change efforts fail are quite simple: management doesn't know what to do and/or gives up too early" (p.122).

This difference between traditional organizations and those who succeed with operations excellence is created through a new model built upon leading organizational cultural transformation at an unprecedented scale. Continuing to plan and implement operational excellence based on traditional models leads to a lack of cultural transformation required to ensure the sustainment of any competitive advantage gained. Pearce and Robinson (2003) in *Strategic Management: Formulation, Implementation, and Control* provide the following:

> The stronger a company's culture and the more that culture is directed toward customers and markets, the less the company uses policy manuals, organization charts, and detailed rules and procedures to enforce discipline and norms. The reason is that the guiding

values inherent in the culture convey in crystal-clear fashion what everybody is supposed to do in most situations. Poorly performing companies often have strong cultures. However, their cultures are dysfunctional, being focused on internal politics or operating by the numbers as opposed to emphasizing customers and the people who make and sell the product. (p. 300)

The successful companies in the future will be ones wise enough to harness the full potential of the entire organization in rapidly changing internally so to remain competitive in the external environment.

New Operations Excellence Strategy Model

Leaders must prepare the way for change while creating an environment that fosters it since resistance to transformational change is natural. Resistance emanates from many sources including old mindsets, habit, compliancy, and fear of the unknown, the desire for the security of the past, career and political power structures.

An essential task of the change leadership process is getting people to think and to act differently. Whatever the individual position of those leading a transformational change journey, there is a general approach that Pietersen (2002) has developed outlining three stages regarding new values and behaviors:

1. To change is to suffer loss – loss of several kinds. We lose certainty, the comfort of the known and the familiar. We lose the sense of competency, financial security, and status that goes along with the existing order of things.

2. Because change involves loss, people must be convinced that the gains will be greater than the losses if they are to embrace change.

3. To succeed, therefore, the driving forces in support of change must be greater than the restraining forces of fear, uncertainty, and doubt. (p.189)

Transformational change must occur at all levels of the organization by distributing leadership roles to engage and empower people to act within established expectations of behavior in support of the strategy and vision. Sullivan and Harper (1996) write that "effective leadership is not about controlling from the top; it is about unleashing the power of people" (p. 115).

In the context of transformation, change leadership is not an art to be practiced by only a few top executives. Although continuous involvement of top executives in major change is a must, leadership should be carried out at all levels of the organization. The leadership at other levels of the organization might be functional and business unit managers, members of the various teams working on accomplishing the change as well as individuals throughout the organization. In operations excellence, everyone must be a leader. It is clear that those individuals heading the transformational journey will need to possess far more than the usual business management skills of finance, marketing and technology application. They must be able to lead individuals into uncharted waters.

Thus, leaders must commit to learning the skills of human behavior and group dynamics including how to influence team processes, activities, norms and values. In the past, many managers have developed effective means for dealing with problems and gaining results, these may be of little use during a transformational journey, and hence there are several new requirements of the transformation change leadership process.

Successful, as well as unsuccessful change journeys show that transformational challenges can not be dealt with in a sustained fashion without strong and ongoing change leadership that involves two concepts. First, the guiding of the organization to deal with constant change while secondly, providing leadership skills to cope with the ramifications of constant change. Pearce and Robinson (2003) point out that "the leadership challenge is to galvanize commitment among people within an organization as well as stakeholders outside the organization to embraced change and implement strategies intended to position the organization to do so" (p.294).

Today, though still greatly concerned with cost, maximizing operational efficiencies, and performance improvement, business leaders must shift their focus to issues of how to build resource capabilities and create structures, processes, and control methods that continuously adapt for competitive advantage. Sullivan and Harper (1996) declare:

> For an enduring organization there is no finite end state, only a journey-always becoming, never being.... A leader must accept these realities and grow the organization to survive and prosper in an ambiguous, uncertain world that makes precise planning a business school exercise. (p.131)

The strategies chosen should allow the business to take advantage of its core competencies relative to opportunities in the external environment. In the new business environment of rapid changes, heightened risk, and uncertainty, developing effective strategies is critical. They prepare executives to face the uncertainties ahead and serve as the focal point for creative thinking about a company's vision and direction. New models that will drive operations excellence must have a greater focus on the basics of what ultimately creates value today; culture, capable resources, and change leadership that ensure that each piece of the business contributes to system wide change. Leadership must view the company as a collection of capabilities, and strategy as a method to learn, focus, align, and sustain improvements.

A current prevailing strategy model is the resource based theory. Traditional strategy models, such as Michael Porter's five forces model, focus on the company's external competitive environment. Most companies do not attempt to look internally for strengths, weakness, opportunities, and threats. In contrast, the resource-based perspective highlights the need for a fit between the external market in which a company operates and its internal capabilities. According to this view, a company's competitive advantage is derived from its ability to assemble and leverage an appropriate combination of resources. Sustainable competitive advantage is achieved by continuously developing existing resources while creating new resources capabilities in support of rapidly changing market conditions.

In contrast to traditional models, the resource based view is founded in the perspective that a firm's internal resources and capabilities are more critical to the determination of strategic action than is the external environment. Instead of focusing on the accumulation of resources necessary to implement the strategy dictated by conditions and constraints in the external environment, the resource based view suggests that a company's unique resources and capabilities provide the basis for strategy. Kaplan and Norton (2001) explain that through research of successful companies they found a common feature in that all:

> Put strategy at the center of its change and management process. By clearly defining the strategy, communicating it consistently, and linking it to the drivers of change, a performance-based culture emerged that linked everyone and every unit to the unique features of the strategy. (p.25)

As outlined in the traditional model section, companies get little value from their annual strategic planning process. To meet new challenges, the planning process should be redesigned to support a strategy that encourages development of internal resource capabilities. Lareau (2000) provides the following concerning change:

The challenge of organizational change is getting

everybody in the organization on-board and moving in a

different direction than the one that's currently being

pursued. In effect, you must change thousands of

expectations, self-fulfilling prophecies and need

fulfillment contingencies as well as hundreds, if not

thousands, of group norms, values and goals. (p.121)

New operations excellence models must have a

stronger focus on the basics of what ultimately creates value

today, resources that are capable, flexible and reliable. New

models must go beyond the simple application of techniques

to foster the creation of organizational culture change

ensuring that each piece of the business contributes to system

wide transformation in an aligned and integrated fashion.

Operations excellence then places an emphasis upon

development and utilization of the company's resources and

capabilities to create the competitive advantage leading to

sustainable value creation for the customer and shareholders.

Cowley and Domb (1997) point out that, "if the capability

required to meet an important objective does not exist, then a creative way to develop or acquire it may be needed. In fact, a breakthrough may be needed at the strategic level" (p.28).

Within the new model, the foundation of operations excellence will consist of change leadership coupled with the implementation of lean manufacturing. While specific techniques provide their benefit by increasing the capabilities of resources through improved structure, processes and control systems the implementation is driven as a complete transformation of the organization culture. Transformation that provides vision with committed leadership who engage the total workforce through actionable improvements, organizational structure alignment and integration for cross functional ownership on the few critical objectives, united with control systems built upon redesigned procedures, policies, and performance metrics.

To accomplish generic strategies, as defined by Porter, of either being the low cost producer or provider of product and services that are differentiated from competitors requires that the organization generate a major focus on the improvement of capabilities and resources throughout. This means a key undertaking to increase the effectiveness and efficiency of the organizations structures, processes, and control mechanisms or as Kaplan and Norton (2001) define, "the essence of strategy is choosing to perform activities differently from competitors so as to provide a unique value proposition" (p. 75).

The creation of resource capability, flexibility, and reliability are the fundamental basis to ensure creation of distinctive competencies in the organization. These organizational changes are the journey to superior performance in quality, efficiency, innovation, and customer responsiveness. Thus, transformation of the organization to operations excellence is the outcome of a business strategy. A strategy that is executed to meet both the dynamics of the changing global markets as well as to put into place an organizational culture of superior performance sustaining competitive advantage. "The core of any business strategy – connecting a company's internal processes to improved outcomes with customers – is the "value proposition" delivered to the customer" (Kaplan & Norton, 2001, p.86).

Leadership must constantly review strategy in order to contend with dynamic competition by allowing experimentation with new concepts, testing, adaptation and building on what is found to be successful especially when trying to re-invent value.   Sullivan and Harper (1996) define this vital aspect of strategy as, "at its essence, strategy is an intellectual construct linking where you are today with where you want to be tomorrow in a substantive, concrete manner" (p.98). Vital in this definition of strategy is the term "intellectual", specifically leadership must have a detailed knowledge of their business systems while utilizing a strategic model that provides structured resource development of maturity. Secondly, leadership must have a through understanding of how to lead change and conduct organization wide transformation. Thus organizational change leadership is a vital link to the future success which is expressed by Hamel and Prahalad (1994) as:

> ...any company that is more of a bystander than a driver on the road to the future will find its structure, values, and skills becoming progressively less attuned to an every changing industry reality. Such a discrepancy between the pace of change in the industry environment and the pace of change in the internal environment spawns the daunting task of organizational transformation. (p.6)

Companies develop their strategic architecture that "identifies the major capabilities to be built, but doesn't specify exactly how they are to be built" (Hamel & Prahalad, 1994, p.108). From this architecture, leaders must create, develop, and foster an environment for organizational change by establishing the strategic intent, structuring the organization to support the strategy, and shape the organization culture to sustain the strategy. Sullivan and Harper, (1996) conclude that:

> The power of a complete strategic architecture lies in the linking of values and vision with deliberate concepts for action that adhere to the critical processes in an organization ... becomes the basis for decentralized execution and empowerment because it gives people a foundation from which to be self-directing. (p.107)

With strategic intent leadership must establish the concepts of "what" and "how" the operations excellence transformation will be achieved.

Thus when leadership selects operations excellence as an integral part of strategy the intent must be clearly understood that in order to achieve sustainable competitive advantage, breakthrough change in the organization culture must occur. Hamel and Prahalad (1994) have written that:

> Strategic intent implies a significant stretch for the organization. Current capabilities and resources are manifestly insufficient to the task. Whereas the traditional view of strategy focuses on the "fit" between existing resources and emerging opportunities, strategic intent creates, by design, a substantial "misfit" between resources and aspirations. (p.129)

The strategic intent must become operations excellence in all facets of the business organization for total alignment and integration of structures, processes, and control methods.

This requires shifting organizational focus to issues of how to build capabilities for growth and productivity, how to attract and retain the best people, how to develop leaders at all levels in the company, and how to lead:

> ...by changing the critical processes – not simply making adjustments at the margin-the leader creates a

pattern, a structure, for doing things differently at the most basic level of the organization. Only by making change at this fundamental level is it possible to effect substantive and enduring transformation. (Sullivan & Harper, 1996, p. 102)

Once the operations excellence strategic intent is conceptualized and prior to the development of the implementation plan there must be vision. The creation of a vision at this early phase of the transformation is imperative to provide scope as to what the future of the business shall look like and the parameters that define this state. To be effective, the vision must have meaning, be understood, and drive focused actions throughout the entire organization. Most importantly, the vision becomes the criteria of consistency linking all action items on the journey to operations excellence into an integrated and aligned implementation plan. This very aspect "becomes the basis of decentralized execution and empowerment because it gives people a foundation from which to be self-directing" (Sullivan and Harper, 1996, p.107).

Of vital importance then to achievement of operations excellence is the vision, a view of what the business will look and function like in the future. Hamel and Prahalad (1994) have written that "creating the future is more challenging than playing catch up, in that you have to create your own road map" (p.22). It is the image that a business must have of its objectives and goals before it sets out to reach them. "A vision must fit the organization for which it was created, and it must be empowering, providing both the leader and the led a tool they can translate into strategy and action that result in real growth and change" (Sullivan & Harper, 1996, p. 88). It describes aspirations for the future, without specifying the means that will be used to achieve those desired ends.

The vision provides focus on the future desired state of the business organization. This desired state creates the ability of the leadership to select only the critical few strategic objectives that truly support the strategic intent. Lareau (2000) declares that in order for operation excellence elements such as lean manufacturing to occur there is first a requirement for visionary leadership, "visionary leadership is the application of a set of beliefs, expectations and direction that focuses everyone in an organization on critical objectives in an effective manner" (p.82).

This aspect is the essence of vision; establishing a base of understanding within leadership and the workforce creating the environment that all individuals have the same clear view as to which initiatives, objectives, and goals must be the focus so that all actions are integrated to achieve consistency. As discussed, in traditional organizations, "each and every employee and department may be working towards conflicting objectives. That's how sub-optimization flourishes; all sorts of enthusiastic people working very hard at different personal visions" (Lareau, 2000, p.166). The vision must effectively describe the future in a way that people can grasp in simple operational terms and be applicable to each individual's role in the organization. At a minimum the vision must:

- Provide the background for change
- Provide a sense of purpose
- Provide a view of success
- Rise above day to day issues

Leadership must define a vision for the desired future and have the ability to articulate that vision in a fashion that develops understanding, builds focus and commitment as well as organization wide ownership. This is particularly important during times of extreme change within the operations. Kotter (1996) describes the roles of vision as:

> In a change process, a good vision serves three important purposes. First, by clarifying the general direction for change....Secondly, it motivates people to take action in the right direction. ...Third, it helps coordinate the actions of different people, even thousand and thousands of individuals, in a remarkably fast and efficient way. (pp. 68-69)

This consistency is what makes a corporation greater than the sum of it parts. "The vision represents a shared expression of the future desired by the members of the organization. It is an essential step toward the creation of unity of purpose in all their endeavors" (Cowley & Domb, 1997, p.67).

By achieving consistency, every individual and each part of the company will be better able to drive with determination toward a common goal that is clear, communicated, and understood by everyone. To energize the workforce towards strategic objectives, visions must be more than a sign on the wall they must become a daily operational lifestyle. Lareau (2000) writes about the importance of change leadership articulating vision "...it is critical that a leader lives the vision him/herself on a minute-by-minute basis" (p. 175). Leadership should live them, be seen living them, and constantly communicate them to their employees.

If the leadership is asking everyone to engage in change that creates stress, the establishment of a clear and consistent vision of what the future will be aids greatly in the organizations understanding and the people through the transformation. For a vision to have any impact on the employees of an organization it has to be conveyed in a dramatic and enduring way. The most effective visions are those that inspire, usually asking employees for the best, the most or the greatest. The vision should drive the organization to stretch in objectives and goals while keeping linkages between the events of today and the vision. Sullivan and Harper (1996) state:

> To be an effective beacon, a vision must describe the future in terms that people can easily grasp and understand. It must incorporate some concept of success that is simple enough for people to understand

in operational terms, that is, they must be able to apply it to their role in the organization, to their job. (p. 79)

Leadership must take the vision once created and understood and begin the relentless communication to the entire organization. Communication of the vision is a vital link from the current level of organizational performance to an anticipated and desired level of future performance. "A vision is "good" or "bad" to the extent that it becomes an accepted, assumed and practiced element of the organizational culture, management system and leadership philosophy" (Lareau, 2000, p.169). Leadership's communication must be in such a fashion to have meaning, clear in specifics, and provide the perception of how each individual can assist in creating the new future. Kotter (1996) points out the key elements of effective communications of vision to be; simplicity, metaphor and analogy, multiple forums, repetition, leadership by example, explanation of seeming inconsistencies, and give and take (p. 90).

Once the vision is firmly understood, leadership determines what vital few breakthrough objectives are required to achieve the strategy. Breakthrough changes are major undertakings that establish new process and systems. Something better, something different, where vision is a long term outlook of what the business will look like after the radical changes and improvements. Leadership must understand and commit to operations excellence that when approached from an organizational transformation standpoint that the breakthrough objective might take several years to achieve.

Operations excellence strategy is then developed, refined, and deployed through a serious of reviews with each succeeding level of the organization through a method called Policy Deployment (also referred to as Strategy Deployment). This process provides a standardized format to ensure that long term vision, three to five year plans, and annual plans are communicated to all levels of the organization in a fashion that develops understanding, buy in, and ownership. This deployment translates the operations excellence intent into meaningful actions developed within the organization specific to each level by individuals that own the processes, aligns the organization structure to support the strategy, and ensures that the focus remains continuous with engaged and committed leadership.

Policy deployment creates the structural support necessary for achievement of operations excellence. Feld (2001) declares that, "the major intent behind policy deployment is to steer an entire organization in the same overall direction. When an entire organization is pulling in the same direction, it is much easier to take corrective action and adjust the course" (p.40). The total organization is aligned to the few key objectives versus the global traditional approach which overburdens the organization with a multitude of objectives and goals that compete for limited resources. Furthermore, the coupling of vision and strategy deployment establishes the integration of the total structure to facilitate the needed support and cross functional ownership of objectives. Total integration is required to ensure that all structural, process and control methods are holistic system wide in approach and effect.

The cascading of the strategy down and up through the organization creates a clear understanding of the strategic intent, specific objectives, and expectations of desired outcomes. This permits input, discussion and buy-in by the various organizational levels as the strategy is being planned and rolled out. The policy deployment process then builds the ownership and commitment by leadership, teams, and individuals that are in position to affect the outcome through changed behaviors; thereby becoming an integral part of change leadership in that the process creates an organization in which all functions act consistently toward a few prioritized breakthrough objectives. As Allen et al. (2001) declare:

> Policy deployment means organizing a company for effectiveness. Without a standardized process by which to coordinate activities, companies can go in many different directions resulting in duplication, conflicting goals, and poor results. (p.219)

The implementation plan is rolled out to the organizational departments through a series of "catch ball" interactions between immediate manager and employees. The objectives are cascaded down a level in which a senior manager will develop with a mid-manager several key objectives with specific goals, such as a departmental increase in productivity by 10% over the next twelve months or a goal to support another department in the achievement of an objective in which integrated ownership is required. Through back and forth catch ball discussions, the managers and employees come to a better understanding of the initiative, the importance of the department's role in achievement, and greater buy in from individuals.

The mid level manager in turns will conduct a similar catch ball session with his or her team members. In continuation of the above example the mid level manager will meet with the supervisors within the department and proceed through the same process of communication, development of objective understanding, and team consensus as to actions and engagement. Specific goals will be agreed upon by all members developing a greater buy in and ownership of the change initiative. The 10% productivity goal for the mid level manager is shared across the various supervisors within the department so that Assembly might be 2%, Paint 2% and Fabrication 6%. This catch ball process will continue till initiatives are communicated and developed down to teams and individual member levels.

In particular, policy deployment accomplishes two vital aspects as a change leadership practice. First, the process is effective at establishing clear understanding of the few key initiatives that will drive breakthrough improvements that are necessary. Secondly, vision, objectives, and critical actions to accomplish are effectively communicated in a manner that creates alignment and integration of all organizational functions with a commonality of purpose. Cowley and Domb (1997) identified a key characteristic of utilization of policy deployment methodology as, "the biggest mistake organizations make is failing to focus on the high-leverage actions that really make a difference in the organization's long term competitiveness" (p. 74).

To facilitate change, provide the guiding leadership in review of progress, align priorities, focus, integration of ownership, and overall support is the role of a Plant Steering Team consisting of senior leadership as well as individuals who provide leadership due to credibility, skill, and respect within the operation. Individually, each member will service as champion or sponsor of various engagement activities. Kotter (1996) reflects on the importance of this team in, "building such a team is always an essential part of the early stages of any effort to restructure, reengineer, or retool a set of strategies" (p. 52).

Kotter (1996) goes on to identify four key characteristics for individuals in this leadership team:

Position power ensures that the right key players are members of the steering team to eliminate barriers to implementation through their level within the organization or their ability to get things done. Team members must have subject matter expertise relevant to the initiative which is vital to make the right decisions. Membership credibility in that each member has a reputation within the organization to gain support and commitment from others, and finally leadership being that the members have proven abilities to inspire and motivated engagement in change (p. 57).

Driving high level transformation requires both the mobilization and continuous application of change leadership throughout all stages of the journey. This entails the ability to translate the strategy to create a sense of urgency and understanding through communications. Leaders must identify the required changes early in the strategic initiative that are required to ensure competitive advantage then develop a sense of urgency throughout the organization founded on why the change is required. Leadership must ensure that the urgency for change is reinforced by a clear perception of operations excellence in addition to well defined expectations and desired outcomes. Vital in this process is the recognition that operations excellence is more than simple implementation of the techniques of lean manufacturing; it is about organizational culture change.

With this alignment and a firm appreciation of the scope of the operations excellence transformation leadership can begin to articulate the message through various communication methods that is meaningful to each team member combined with defining how individually each member will be affected and how their actions can affect the future of the organization. This becomes in essence the most difficult and crucial challenge for leaders of major change, the process of motivating and inspiring people not just to do what you want, but to want what you want.

Meeting this challenge takes far more than crafting vision statements and making speeches. It requires building into people the comprehension, commitment, and capabilities needed to successfully implement change. Comprehension involves getting people to understand what the change will involve and why it is necessary. Commitment entails getting people to take ownership of, or accept responsibility for the change. While capabilities means putting in place the processes necessary to build the knowledge, skills, actions and systems to create and sustain change. Lareau (2000) writes, "in order for an employee to be part of a true pursuit of continuous improvement, he/she must understand exactly how his/her performance on critical job tasks is measured and exactly what the level of current performance is" (p. 85).

Before they will accept change, the workforce must first understand what is to be accomplished and then be convinced of the need for it. They must be given the facts about the situation and help in understanding issues such as the marketplace and economic factors facing the company, the level of improvements needed to become competitive again and the new organizational standards expected. Communications must have substance and meaningful information; it can not be simple boiler plate.

Development of a communication plan should focus on the three levels of the organization; first line employees, mid management, executive level, tailoring the content and subject matter for each group. Feld (2001) presents the following methodology:

> When presenting the plan to the different levels within the organization, make sure the following four questions are answered as a part of the communications:
>
> 1. Why are we changing?
> 2. What are we changing?
> 3. Where are we now?
> 4. What's in it for me? (p.25)

Why are we changing? The communication process must provide clear descriptions of the changes being made and the linkage to the overall direction (vision) for the operation. The outline should give meaning to each level so that individually there is understanding of the new expectations and work environment. This must include specific metrics where applicable to provide greater clarification followed by sessions giving an overview and details as appropriate to individuals of the implementation plan. The plan coupled with initial discussions of new expectations must provide a baseline of the current situation within the business while developing the perspective within individuals for clarification of urgency and the scope of the initiative. Finally, what is in it for me? Communications must create complete understanding for each individual of where they fit into the new organization, how the changes will impact their specific roles and responsibilities, as well as outlining what gains will be made and how these benefit the individual, team, and organization.

Throughout this communication process it is essential to provide a story line of why the operations excellence changes are needed and what changes will be included. Leadership should always make this from the point of view of what it means to that individual or particular team providing insight from the affected individual's perspective. Kaplan and Norton (2001) have concluded that organizations conducting operations excellence transformation "require that employees understand the strategy and conduct their day-to-day business in a way that contributes to the success of that strategy. This is not top-down direction. This is top-down communication" (p.12).

Communications must be constantly occurring within the organization based on both formal and informal formats using verbal and written methods. Formal methods might include mass meetings, small groups, newsletters, postings, etc. where aspects for the urgency and change will be outlined. Informal communication such as walking through areas of the operation talking to individuals one on one about the changes and expectations can be one of the most effective methods. These informal methods are very successful typically more than formal methods since individuals are at ease which creates the environment that permits listening and understanding.

One critical element of communication for leadership is that of physical communication. Stating that the plant must be cleaned up and setting the expectation that litter will be picked up by all employees, yet a leader walking through the plant and stepping over litter on the floor. As a leader, every action is viewed and watched by others in great detail to see if the leader is walking the walk or simply providing the talk. As a leader the physical communication is through actions that are viewed by others and reinforce the desired expectations, values and behaviors. Sullivan and Harper (1996) point out that:

By sponsoring specific activities and events designed to illustrate and test the new paradigm, a leader encourages similar behavior in others, causing them to look beyond today and participate in creating the new organization. (p. 187)

Without a well conceived communication process, it is very unlikely that the workforce and leadership will become committed to and stay committed to the change. To successfully achieve this goal, it is not enough to preach a new gospel once at the start of the journey. Rather, continuous communication is necessary throughout its entirety. One of the main communication tasks of leaders is making the vision of the future real in the minds of the people who are asked to accept, support, contribute to and live with the change. The use of stories, videos, images, symbols and language can be powerful ways to make the future come alive.

Once the sense of urgency is created, vision established, and communication process in place, the organizational structure needs alignment to emphasize and support strategically critical activities. The organizational structure should facilitate the coordination and integration of all business functions to maximize their support in a way to leverage resources through focused efforts. Key to this structure is the removal of functional barriers by creating an organization with no boundaries·

- Ensuring common understanding and urgency of priorities
- Clarifying responsibilities among managers and organizational units
- Empowering and pushing authority lower in the organization
- Addressing problems in coordination and communication
- Gaining the personal commitment to a shared vision

In the new operations excellence model the organization is flat, redeploying the intermediary management roles. These roles are taken up by the development and use of such positions as team leaders, cell leaders, value stream leaders, etc. to conduct the daily as well as change activities.

Managers will be redeployed into roles of facilitators, mentors, and coaches in effort to provide direct leadership guidance.

Beyond the redeployment of mid management into new roles, another key concept in this structure that builds upon the active engagement of individuals in natural work groups coupled with empowerment. Within this team is a small group of individuals sharing a set of common operations bound together through expectations, objectives, values, concerns and opportunities. This permits a teaming of individuals who have a shared understanding of the operations excellence intent and most knowledgeable with specific operations to develop and execute improvement actions. Assigned to each team is a leader skilled in facilitation, coaching, and trained on various aspects of business and lean manufacturing required for successful team application of the techniques, resourcefulness, and culture change.

Two types of team are often deployed in transformational journeys; temporary teams for supporting the numerous goals and tasks of the change process (for example, change management and process design teams), and permanent teams that run and support the new processes resulting from the change effort and which become the foundation of the new organization. Whether temporary or permanent, successful teams have several characteristics that support the transformational effort:

- They have a clear vision that drives the team's thinking and action.
- Team purpose is aligned with individuals' goals, visions and norms while conflicting views are managed as a source of creativity.
- There is open communication with regular, fact-based feedback given and received amongst team members.
- They have shared understanding of individual roles and accountabilities.

Further structural ownership and support must be gained through the development and use of cross functional teams and individual contributors. Assignment of initiatives to members and functions outside the normal roll brings greater organizational integration to the strategy, expanding the knowledge base for the endeavor and creates the ownership necessary for commitment.

Fundamental to this operations excellence transformation is the learning, development and capabilities of intangible resources, both human and technology. Kaplan and Norton (2001) have developed a three category perspective that goes beyond the traditional development of strategic competencies and technologies with a focus upon the "climate for action: The cultural shifts needed to motivate, empower, and align the workforce behind the strategy" (p.93). Learning the new way of working, the new behavioral habits and skills, requires the leaders to take a holistic approach to the learning process to achieve sustainable competitive advantage.

Leadership must go beyond the policy deployment, vision, communication process, and organizational structure driving change through the difficult work of modifying, teaching, creating, and demonstrating the new values, expectations and behaviors desired. Pietersen (2002) declares, "the company then faces one of the greatest leadership challenges: the need to change an ingrained corporate culture in response to a changed strategy" (p.154).

As individuals become more aware of these new behaviors and committed to the need for change they begin to find the new methods more rewarding and self satisfying.

Over time, given proper development and coaching individuals and teams will establish these changed behaviors as the new standards of operations. These new shared norms then shape the work environment becoming the foundation for a transformed organizational culture. "Organizational culture is the set of important assumptions (often unstated) that members of an organization share in common....an intangible yet ever present theme that provides meaning, direction, and the basis for action" (Pearce & Robinson, 2003, p.298).

Leadership for operations excellence then requires the forming of new expectations, values and behaviors around a core of elements including:

- Focus upon the strategic intent.
- Create a common view of the organization that is to be created, the vision of the future state.
- Untiring communication to build understanding, set the new expectations, and open dialog for constructive discussions.
- Institutionalize desired behaviors through example, feedback, rewards, and assessments.

Transformation of a traditional culture to one that supports operations excellence requires breakthrough changes on a total business system scale. The challenge becomes the understanding and ability of leadership to target the desired behaviors throughout the organization; behaviors that clearly define and set the expectation for the new structure, processes, and control methods that achieve extraordinary levels of performance from distinctive competencies, the essence of true sustainable competitive advantage.

Leadership must be strong enough, knowledgeable enough, committed enough to be willing to take on the soft stuff associated with breakthrough culture change developing maturity in resource capabilities leading to distinctive competencies. Simple application of techniques such as those associated with lean manufacturing only provides incremental improvements. Pietersen (2002) has written that the critical aspect of breakthrough versus incremental change as, "you will never be a long term winner through continuous improvement alone. You must also seek and create breakthrough changes" (p.33).

The leaders of change must learn how to implement change, how to influence, guide, coach and find the right balance between push and pull. Those affected by change must first be convinced that both organization and individual change is necessary before they will be willing to accept the need to learn something new. The natural reaction of someone who is confronted with the imperative to change his or her environment and way of working is to ask themselves questions such as: Who am I? What will be my role? What will my reputation be? Can I cope? The motivation for these questions is rooted in the natural human need for being in a stable and predictable environment. If the answers to these questions are not clear or fully understood, then people may feel threatened, anxious and fearful.

Changing behavior and attitudes quickly requires an accelerated process of learning of which a crucial component is creating a framework to enable people to act in new ways and to see, feel and appreciate the results obtained from new ways of working. It is through this experience that, for a majority of people, learning will best occur. The learning process itself will need to be structured to enable and promote the desired positive and sustainable changes of behavior.

This is an important responsibility of the change leaders and must be designed to take into account the desired results as well as the unique characteristics of the company's culture and the individuals involved. Earlier, the importance of communications was the topic and why the clear understanding of the need for change must be developed in the workforce on an individual basis. People have to acknowledge that a change is necessary.

This cannot be done by just stating that the company is in trouble. Employees also need to understand the reasons for change, which often requires intense, candid and trusting communication of the forces and intent for change. This cannot be achieved by a single announcement but rather through a process of unfreezing, or unlearning of old values, behaviors, beliefs and norms that are no longer appropriate. This part of the learning process takes some time which in the traditional organization is an aspect little appreciated in lieu of rapid results.

Once people are convinced that change is necessary, they must still be convinced that they themselves must change by addressing the why must I change? Here, the change leader has to discover what motivates individuals to learn and behave in new ways. Issues of fear and job security must be dealt with as well. People learn best and easier in a psychologically safe environment where they are allowed to make mistakes yet not lose face. Creating an environment that is purposely structured to enable people to experiment with new ways of working will best promote learning and relieves the individual stress associated with; will I be able to change?

Furthermore, a key element for change leadership that is often overlooked is the alignment and integration of procedures, measurement, and performance reviews to support the new operations excellence strategy. Each must be completely aligned to establish and reinforce the desire expectation, values, and behaviors sought in the new culture.

Transformational change requires measurement criteria and systems that take into account the objectives that support the new redesigned way of working, which may change dramatically based on the level of breakthrough initiatives. Measurement is a vital aspect for creation of focus and used to align with support through feedback on performance and progress of the change effort. Leaders introducing new strategies intended to achieve breakthroughs need measures of performance that are far more robust than traditional, short term financial indicators like return-on-investment, sales growth and net income.

These measurement and performance processes are complicated by two major requirements: the need to determine the right types of measures and to align them with the goals and objectives of the strategy as well as the necessity to apply them in ways that positively influence the behavior and performance of people. Pietersen (2002) confirms the complexity and lack of understanding of the importance of performance measurement in that, "it is surprising how often a firm will try to introduce a new strategy while continuing to measure and reward the behaviors that supported the old strategy" (p.140).

Leadership must establish metrics and key performance indicators that reflect the desired expectations and reinforce the behaviors, values and norms in the new organization. Metrics must be developed at the lowest level possible by individuals who will monitor the metric, have control of the process, and the ability to take active involvement to correct deficiencies. Feld (2001) states:

If people cannot describe their measure of performance, do not own that measure, do not report on the measure, nor understand cause and effect relative to the measure, then it is unrealistic to expect the measure to improve. (p.42)

This will include methods for feedback up and down the hierarchy that must be put into place and acted upon with committed support. Regular reviews must be conducted at all levels in a timely fashion to understand progress, to implement countermeasure to correct issues where applicable and ensure the appropriate use of resources to achieve targeted outcomes. Lareau (2000) is progressive in the thought that, "feedback to employees should occur on at least a weekly basis (daily is better). In addition, employees must be given the resources, coaching, support and training that will enable them to take the necessary actions to move the metrics in a positive direction" (p.85).

Developing new measures of individual performance is another important challenge facing leaders of transformational change. This often requires creating an entirely new set of criteria for measurement and assessment. Most companies have traditionally applied narrow measures of individual performance such as performance to plan for individually specific tasks and projects. Operations excellence however, requires devising new measurement schemes that also take into account factors such as the knowledge, skills, attitudes and values that characterize the new culture. Kaplan and Norton (2001) state "managers evaluated by short-term financial measures will manage to those measures, and likely short change new initiatives for growth, customer focus, innovation, and employee empowerment" (p.343).

Recognition and reward systems have long been standard instruments of business. Managers in some countries, such as the United States and the United Kingdom, have relied on them, particularly financial incentives and compensation, to motivate people to act in specific ways or to achieve particular goals. Most of these systems are designed for use within a functionally or hierarchically oriented business environment. As organizations redefine how they are organized and carry out work, however, they must change how they recognize and reward people.

From a leadership point of view, two major challenges can be observed concerning performance and metric review during transformational change. First is the task of developing the right types and levels of new measurement and assessment. A second challenge is gaining acceptance of the new measures and measurement systems throughout the organization. A good measurement system reflects a balance of several characteristics to get people to accept and behave according to them that creates a positive reinforcing effect if they are tied to actions that impact the work process and well thought out.

New operations excellence models must stress the combination of the application of lean manufacturing techniques with the critical aspects of change leadership. Change leadership that provides a fundamental breakthrough in the organizational culture, one that is aligned and integrated to fully support the strategy through new structures, processes, and control methods. An organizational culture that is transformed from traditional models creating superior performance that is sustainable through distinctive competencies of resources.

Operations Excellence as Sustainable Competitive Advantage

The overall objective of the operations excellence strategic intent is the establishment of increased value for both the customer and the shareholder through transformation of structures, processes and control mechanisms creating a new organizational culture. This is accomplished through an effective combination of tangible and intangible resources that is flexible, reliable and capable thereby creating superior performance in efficiency, quality, innovation, and customer service.

New models for operations excellence must include strong elements of organization change leadership from senior level through cell/team leaders. Inclusive in the model will be an extensive level of communication by the leadership team supported with a vision that creates focus on a few key breakthrough initiatives building alignment and integration of all business functions. This focus is heightened through an organization structure that directly corresponds to the strategy deployment. Finally, the model must satisfy the need for system closure with feedback loops, metrics, and other applicable control procedures. These basic requirements are in addition to the application of the various techniques of lean manufacturing.

The opportunity for the company to sustain its competitive advantage is determined by capabilities of two kinds; distinctive capabilities and reproducible capabilities, and their unique combination created by synergy. Distinctive capabilities are the characteristics within the organization that cannot be replicated by competitors, or can only be replicated with great difficulty hence they are the basis of sustainable competitive advantage. Examples of distinctive capabilities include: patents, exclusive licenses, strong brands, effective leadership, teamwork, knowledge and organizational culture.

Reproducible capabilities such as technical processes, product design, financial, and marketing capabilities are those that can be bought or created by competitors and thus by themselves cannot be a source of competitive advantage. Distinctive competencies must be supported by an appropriate set of complementary reproducible capabilities to enable the business to position its competitive advantage in the market. These reproducible capabilities are typically techniques and applications of lean manufacturing such as; SMED, Kanban, or TPM. Each of these techniques provides great improvement in processes for increased effectiveness and efficiencies driving up profitability through value to the customer. Yet, each of these can be copied by competitors, the distinctive competencies are created when combined with change leadership for the development and maturity of structure, processes and controls which define the new organizational culture.

Competitive advantage exist when a business is able to deliver the same benefits as competitors but at a lower cost, or deliver benefits that exceed those of competing products. Thus, a competitive advantage enables the firm to create superior value for its customers and superior profits for itself. Sustainable competitive advantage allows the maintenance and continuous improvement of the businesses competitive position in the market. According to this view, a company's competitive advantage comes from its ability to assemble and exploit an appropriate combination of resources. Sustainable competitive advantage is achieved by continuously creating new resources and capabilities in response to rapidly changing market conditions (Appendix A, Figure #4).

This brings the transformation to focus upon capability. This is the company's ability to utilize its resources effectively. This strikes at the very foundation of the company in its policies, procedures, methods and processes that are used to achieve objectives. Capabilities therefore are intangible in that they represent the way the company conducts business through the utilization of its resources. Through continued use, capabilities become stronger and more difficult for competitors to understand and imitate hence a distinctive competency.

In order to develop a competitive advantage the company must have resources and capabilities that are superior to those of its competitors. Kaplan and Norton (2001) write that successful "organizations recognize that competitive advantage comes more from the intangible knowledge, capabilities, and relationships created by employees than from investments in physical assets and access to capital" (p.3). These intangible resources are specific assets of the company that can reduce a cost or create differentiation advantage that other businesses will have difficulty in establishing.

Each organization is a collection of unique resources and capabilities that provide the basis for achievement of strategy and the primary source of gains in profitability and productivity. In current competitive environments, businesses must be continuously evolving resource capabilities that are flexible, capable, and reliable. True differences in a business' competitive performance are driven primarily by its unique resources and capabilities rather than by the industry's external characteristics.

A distinction exists between resources and capabilities that should be outlined for clarification. Companies may have numerous resources available in new equipment, a new plant, large workforce, etc. yet this very company may not have the organizational capabilities required to operate effectively and efficiently, thereby under utilizing those resources. Resources are more often thought of as tangible inputs into a business' production process, such as capital, equipment, material and manpower (strictly numbers). Yet, in the new operations excellence model, internal intangible resources such as the skills of individual employees, patents, leadership, and organizational culture provide capabilities. Focusing and aligning resources on the few key objectives increases effectiveness through resourcefulness. It is through the synergy and collective abilities that resources become distinctive competencies, the foundation of sustainable competitive advantage.

A distinctive competency is the capacity for a set of resources to interactively perform a process which through continuous refinement becomes stronger and more difficult for competitors to understand and copy. It is this ability to perform better than competitors using distinctive and difficult to replicate set of business attributes that represents the identity of the business as perceived by both employees and the customers. Operations excellence then becomes the basis of superior performance by impacting the overall capability of the organization. When the development and implementation approach follows new models incorporating various lean manufacturing techniques with organizational culture change, total transformation occurs.

Technology, products, marketing methods, and lean manufacturing can be copied by competitors. No one, however, can match a highly engaged, motivated workforce that is passionately committed to the vision of operations excellence. The strength of the organization's culture is one of the most fundamental competitive advantages. People are a company's most important asset yet at the same time, the most underutilized resource. The workforce is the repository of knowledge and skill that serves as the foundation of operations excellence culture. A well led and highly motivated workforce is critical to the development and execution of strategies, especially in today's faster paced, more perplexing world, where top management alone can no longer assure competitiveness.

Business must have access to the right set of people to get to the right decisions quickly, to distribute responsibility, and to be at the leading edge of competitive performance. A new operations excellence model requires individuals possessing both business skills and a greater level of people skills. Within the operation the organization must establish a partnership between leadership and employees that forms the bonds of understanding of how they benefit as the company benefits. Meanwhile, learning and knowledge must foster understanding that is used through empowerment to make decisions or take actions that are important to the company. As opposed to data and information, knowledge is defined by its use and its relevance to work at actionable levels. It should be linked to the building blocks of how the organization creates value, especially unique know how and capabilities.

This know how is applied within the organization both explicitly and implicitly. Explicit knowledge can be easily written down (for example, patents, formulas, or an engineering schematic), and can create competitive advantage, though its life cycle in competitive markets is increasingly brief since it can be easily replicated by others.

Implicit knowledge is far less tangible and is deeply embedded into an organization's operating practices. It is often called organizational culture which includes relationships, norms, values, and standard operating procedures. Implicit comprises the hidden reasons of why people do what they do through the unconscious beliefs, perceptions, thoughts and feelings. An example of an implicit underlying assumption could be "unless I have the stock in my own warehouse, I have no control over it."

Because culture is much harder to define and copy, it can be a sustainable source of competitive advantage. Organizational psychologists call this aspect of the business system the organizational culture comprised of; values, beliefs, basic assumptions, and norms which impact the behavior of both individuals and teams. The most important implication of this view for leaders is that successful change of culture can only occur if consistent change is implemented to affect all individual and group behavioral. For example, changing organizational structures, implementing SMED, or posting a new metric will not be enough to modify the culture of an organization.

Often, the true barrier to progress of transformational change lies in the upfront failure of management with the violation of underlying assumptions which makes individuals feel unsafe and threatened creating reaction through hidden or outright resistance to the change. Basic assumptions however, are not easy to identify and define, and the practice of dealing with them is still very immature both in traditional organizations and business schools. Managers tend to overlook human behavior and group dynamics as the soft stuff preferring to focus only on the hard technical stuff, even though dealing with the soft stuff indeed is the only way to implement a change of organizational culture that is sustainable.

This organizational behavior framework provides evidence that transformational change cannot be achieved unless sufficient effort is devoted to dealing with the so called soft human resources issues. For transformational change to be successful in a corporate situation, the behavior of individuals who support the new way of working must change. Without a sustainable change of behavior within the workforce comprising an organization, newly invented processes, systems and structures will likely not provide the intended result.

In terms of operations excellence the prime example of sustainable competitive advantage is Toyota. Upon examining Toyota operations, they have typical resources such as any U.S. automotive company with; plants, equipment, number of workforce employed, but what Toyota has that sets them apart from the competition is their capabilities in their utilization of those resources. Toyota has developed their manufacturing system to a level of distinctive competency better known as the TPS. This capability is what companies benchmarking Toyota hope to implement at their operation. What gets over looked in the strategies of companies looking to establish competitive advantage such as Toyota is that the organizational culture *is* the fundamental competitive advantage; the strength of an organizations culture is the foundation of competitive advantages. If the company can build and preserve an adaptive culture where employees are passionately committed and pursue the organization's vision then it is positioned for success.

Today, competitive advantage must be built upon both the resources and capabilities forming the distinctive competencies of the organization and must constantly be reinvented. Business leaders have been confronted with a barrage of fads and strategies over the last decade including, re-engineering, TQM, JIT, lean manufacturing, and six sigma; all promising to increase the level of performance. Many of these panaceas however, failed to deliver the performance improvements promised or expected.

Operations excellence as a sustainable competitive advantage can only be achieved by continuously developing both existing and creating new resources and capabilities in response to rapidly changing market conditions. It is an advantage that enables business to survive against its competition over a long period of time.

CHAPTER 3: METHODOLOGY

Approach

Research for this study was largely draw upon the utilization of surveys and interviews coupled with historical findings. The following outlines the structure and intent of the research methodology.

All surveys are conducted on-line through the services of Advanced Survey (www.advancedsurvey.com). Advanced Survey is a web based provider of survey creation, formatting, data collection, storage, and analysis. This service and web site are provided through a partnership with the, *I Six Sigma* web site (www.isixsigma.com) which specializes in information, training, and best practices for six sigma based initiatives.

Survey #1

A web link for this survey was sent to a total of fifty businesses representing manufacturing and services. The manufacturing sector is divided into thirty nine businesses and the services sector includes eleven participants. Details on the breakdown of these sectors are included in the section titled *Database of Study*.

The survey question asked of the participants is:

> *From the list below of grand strategies identify the one (1) initiative that your company has placed emphasis upon as its priority.* (Appendix B, Figure #24)

The intent is to identify the importance of operations excellence philosophies such as lean manufacturing and six sigma in business.

Survey #2

Participants of Survey #1 who select lean manufacturing or six sigma as a business priority were asked to proceed to Survey #2. The question addressed is:

> *Implementation of the Lean Manufacturing and/or Six Sigma initiatives has reached what level of*

developmental maturity in the organization. (Appendix
B, Figure #25).

The survey intent is to determine of those businesses
implementing operations excellence as a strategic initiative,
what level of sustainable achievement has been reached.

Survey #3

Participants of Survey #2 who select; no sustainment of
results, no improvement results gained, or did not complete
the implementation are asked to proceed to Survey #3. These
participants were asked the question:

*If sustainment of, or improvements have not been
gained from implementing lean manufacturing or six
sigma select the top four barriers applicable.* (Appendix
B, Figure #26)

The intent of this survey is to identify the top barriers or issue
that limit the implementation in a way that ensures lack of

sustainment, not gaining desired results, or not being able to complete the implementation as expected.

<u>Survey #4</u>

This survey was sent to two groups. The first being top senior level executives of a business, the second group, being middle management down to the employees. The survey (Appendix B, Figure #27) consists of fifteen questions concerning elements of change leadership and organizational culture. Each question provides responses of:

- *Not established*
- *Initial steps*
- *Somewhat established*
- *Established*
- *Institutionalized*

The intent of the survey is to establish within each group the level of attainment or implementing of the element in question. Example:

Leadership provides focus and structure to ensure sustainment of change.

Participants from both groups have the same question, same potential responses and the same open criteria to rate achievement of the element based on their organizations level of effectiveness of how well the element has been put into place.

A comparison of the survey answers from the two groups will be made to identify any divergence concerning the perceived level of attainment.

Data Gathering Method

The research comprising this study makes use of both *Descriptive Survey Method* and *Historical/Case Study*. A large portion of the baseline data was based upon descriptive survey methods.

Target selection for study groups includes the two areas of manufacturing and services. The surveys were constructed utilizing the web based resources of Advance Survey (www.advancedsurvey.com). All records and data are stored and compiled via the on-line source. Invitations to participate in the survey were sent via web link to prospective respondents.

The second method employed in conducting the research was historical/case study. Using input from first hand experience and knowledge gained from working in business environments that are actively engaged in launching operations excellence. This experience is coupled with the wealth of information available commercially in the form of books, seminars, and consulting services having expanded upon numerous endeavors of implementing operations excellence and its various techniques.

Database of Study

Participants (50 invited) cover both industry and services in the following breakdown. Manufacturing sectors for pharmaceutical, automotive, steel, telecommunications, and consumer products includes:

- Fortune 500 businesses; Honeywell International Inc., Eaton Corp., Procter & Gamble, Delphi Corp., Caterpillar Inc., Merck & Co. Inc., Newell

Rubbermaid Inc., Unocal Corp., Danaher, Rockwell Automation Inc., Tenneco Automotive Inc. , Parker-Hannifin Corp., Cummins, Nucor, Eli Lilly and Co.

- International Companies; Wal-Mart Stores Inc., Hewlett-Packard Co., Intel Corp., Ford Motor Co., Sun Microsystems, E.I. du Pont de Nemours, Visteon Corp., Whirlpool Corp., Dana Corp., Textron Inc., Ingersoll Rand Corp., Campbell Soup Co., Rohm and Haas Co.,

- Domestic Operations. Rexnord Industries, Kokomo Springs Co., Deroyal Industries, Dixie Box Co., Bull Run Metal Fabrication, Funk Manufacturing Co., Hobart Cabinet Co., Precision Manufacturing Co. Inc. Hartzell Manufacturing Co. Inc., Rittal Corp., Gerstner & Sons,

The final participants represent services of banking, insurance, and health care include:

- Cardinal Health Inc., Wells Fargo & Co., Bank One Corp., Cendant Corp., Nationwide Mutual Insurance Co., Lincoln National Corp., Triad Hospitals Inc.,

Kindred Healthcare Inc., Caremark Rx Inc., U.S. Bancorp, Rite Aid Corp.,

In conjunction with the surveys, personal interviews were conducted with various management and employee level individuals engaged in operations excellence to determine their views on implementation methods and deployment models. The study also used case studies of previous employers that are actively engaged in rolling out and implementing lean manufacturing. Many organizations have developed operations excellence manuals or programs utilizing strategy models relying heavily upon specific techniques. Their success and failures have been participated in, observed, audited at levels including team member, individual contributor, and senior manager.

Finally, there exist a multitude of books published on the subject providing ample background and detailed example on the benefits as well as the applicable specifics of techniques such as TPM, SMED, Kanban, etc.

Validity of Data

The use of on-line web based survey services offered through Advanced Survey (www.advancedsurvey.com) provides an independent clearing house for data collection and storage. Upon completion and publishing of the survey by the author, the survey content, structure, and data collected were secured and could not be altered even by the author. This includes a warning that is issued during the publishing phase of the survey creation that clearly identifies that once published, the survey can not be altered in order to maintain validity.

Participants were sent an invitation to participate in the survey which contains the web link to the site, as well as the log in survey number. Participants at their leisure could sign in to the particular survey of choice, complete the questions, the session is closed out, and the answers provided are logged into the database and compiled.

Advanced Survey compiles data such as:

- Number of participants completing the survey.
- Graphic display of the data.

- Breakdown per questions reflecting the count and percentage answered for each individual's choice per question.

Access to results data is via password log in by the author. The author then has ability to review the summary reports on-line or print to hard copy for file.

Originality and Limitations

Throughout the last decade and early into the new millennium, companies have placed a large priority upon strategies driving cost reductions and process improvement such as operations excellence. Based upon this emphasis, the market has been overwhelmed with business literature, seminars, and professional consulting firms offering expertise on what companies should do without explaining how to do it. What is missing in all the business hype and rhetoric on lean manufacturing is how to go about implementing operations excellence in a fashion that creates an organization with distinctive competencies. Competencies rooted in resources such as man, machine, material, and methods that are adaptive and capable of sustaining true competitive advantage.

This transformation effort requires knowledge of "how" that goes beyond the specific techniques of incremental improvements to breakthrough abilities based on the learning organization. Research and identification of an integrated approach to operations excellence and organization transformation are lacking. This field remains an unexplored area of enormous potential for businesses who truly seek sustainable competitive advantage versus the short lived improvements, failed implementation attempts, and non sustained performance results.

This researcher has been engaged as a senior manager at five major international companies over the past fourteen years. Of these, only one has followed an integrated model that ensures that the operations excellence deployment encompasses change leadership and organizational culture development. This immersion into failed attempts has provided first hand experience and knowledge of the importance of this study, the identification of repeated barriers to successful development and a model to overcome these.

Based upon this experience of repeated failures with companies actively engaged in implementation, coupled with the overall low success rate in business and industry, and the abundance of material dedicated each year to the techniques of lean manufacturing, has lead to the proposal of a new integrated operations excellence transformation model.

Summary

Research conducted during this study relied upon survey data as well as historical and actual case study information. The intent was to determine the level of successful implementation of operations excellence, identification of any constraints or barriers to implementation, and the establishment of change leadership roles that are critical to deployment.

The data gathering method made use of the services provided by Advanced Survey (www.advancedsurvey.com). Services provided include the creation, formatting, and posting of surveys via internet access. Data collection and correlation was provided as a service with basic statistical percentages captured per question answer with graphical display. Furthermore, Advanced Survey provides independent data storage and validity through publishing criteria that protect surveys from modification or data alteration.

The data base of the study included fifty participants representing industry and services. The groups were sub divided to provide representation of major industrial and services sectors. Industry included pharmaceutical, telecommunications, consumer goods, and automotive, while services included health care, banking and insurance businesses.

CHAPTER 4: DATA ANALYSIS

Approach

The data gathered during this research utilized the services provided by Advanced Survey.Com (www.advancedsurvey.com). Advanced Survey provides web hosting for the creation and collection of data related to user defined surveys. Each survey was sent to participants via web link to which the participants were invited to log into the Advanced Survey web site using a specifically designated survey number. Once logged into the site and the appropriate survey, participants answer each question and upon completion the information gathered was input to the hosted database. Advanced Survey provided the basic statistical data gathering ensuring that each question was answered and for each of the possible choices the percentage as well as actual count of those who answered was captured. This same information is displayed graphically by a bar graph representation per question.

Database of the Study

Participants for this study were identified and selected for a total population of fifty businesses. Participants cover both industry and services in the following breakdown. Manufacturing sectors for pharmaceutical, automotive, steel, telecommunications, and consumer products includes:

- Fortune 500 businesses; Honeywell International Inc., Eaton Corp., Procter & Gamble, Delphi Corp., Caterpillar Inc., Merck & Co. Inc., Newell Rubbermaid Inc., Unocal Corp., Danaher, Rockwell Automation Inc., Tenneco Automotive Inc. , Parker-Hannifin Corp., Cummins, Nucor, Eli Lilly and Co.

- International Companies; Wal-Mart Stores Inc., Hewlett-Packard Co., Intel Corp., Ford Motor Co., Sun Microsystems, E.I. du Pont de Nemours, Visteon Corp., Whirlpool Corp., Dana Corp., Textron Inc., Ingersoll Rand Corp., Campbell Soup Co., Rohm and Haas Co.,

- Domestic Operations. Rexnord Industries, Kokomo Springs Co., Deroyal Industries, Dixie Box Co., Bull

Run Metal Fabrication, Funk Manufacturing Co.,
Hobart Cabinet Co., Precision Manufacturing Co.
Inc. Hartzell Manufacturing Co. Inc., Rittal Corp.,
Gerstner & Sons,

The balance of final participants represents services of
banking, insurance, and health care including:

- Cardinal Health Inc., Wells Fargo & Co., Bank One
  Corp., Cendant Corp., Nationwide Mutual Insurance
  Co., Lincoln National Corp., Triad Hospitals Inc.,
  Kindred Healthcare Inc., Caremark Rx Inc., U.S.
  Bancorp, Rite Aid Corp.,

Survey #1 respondents numbered thirty four out of the original
fifty invited. Within the structure of the survey, subgroups of the active
participants could not be identified since respondents where
anonymous. Participants for Survey # 4 included 46 out of 70
senior/executive level managers invited to participate. While Survey #
5 included 61 out of the 70 mid level managers through shop floor
workforce invited to participate.

Data Gathering Method

<u>Survey #1</u>

The intent of this survey was to identify the top grand strategy being employed within the participants operations. The survey consisted of one question:

From the list below of grand strategies identify the one (1) initiative that your company has placed emphasis upon as its priority.

- *Product Innovation*
- *Market Growth*
- *Greater Customer Service*
- *Lean Manufacturing*
- *Acquisition/Divesting*
- *Supply Chain Management*
- *Six Sigma*
- *Share Technology*
- *Total Quality Management*

From the original fifty participants invited to the survey a response was received from a total of thirty four. From the responses, the top three answers by count and percentage are:

Initiative	Count	Percentage
Lean Manufacturing	9	26.47%
Market Growth	8	23.53%
Six Sigma	7	20.59%

TABLE 1 Top Strategic Initiatives

Of the thirty four participants a combined 47.06% have prioritized operations excellence techniques of lean manufacturing and six sigma as the emphasis of strategy. Operations excellence as a strategic initiative ranked twice that of the nearest initiative which was market growth.

Participants that selected lean manufacturing or six sigma where asked to proceed to Survey # 2.

Survey #2

Based upon an emphasis placed on lean manufacturing and six sigma these participants were asked to progress from Survey #1 to assess the level of implementation maturity the organization has reached in its operations excellence endeavor. Survey #2 consists of one question as follows:

Implementation of the Lean Manufacturing and/or Six Sigma initiatives has reached what level of developmental maturity in the organization.

- *Sustaining results after 12 months*
- *Sustaining results for less than 12 months*
- *Not sustaining results*
- *No improvement results gained*
- *Did not complete the implementation*

Of the sixteen participants who selected lean manufacturing and six sigma in Survey #1, twelve progressed to Survey #2 for completion. From the responses, the top three answers by count and percentage are:

Maturity Level	Count	Percentage
Not sustaining results	6	50.00%
No improvement results gained	3	25.00%
Sustaining results for less than 12 months	2	16.67%

TABLE 2 Sustainability

Of the sixteen participants, a total of 12 responded. 0 claimed the ability to sustain results after a period of 12 months while the greatest percentage, 50% of participants claimed that the organization was not sustaining results. Only 2 (16.67%) were claiming performance results sustained from operations excellence, yet this sustainment had been for less than 12 months at the time of the survey. Finishing out the count, 25% reflected that the organization had no improvement results gained and 8.33% answered that they did not complete the implementation. Participants that selected not sustaining results, no improvement results gained, or did not complete the implementations were asked to proceed to Survey # 3.

<u>Survey #3</u>

Participants who selected "no sustained operations excellence or failed to complete the initiative" were asked to proceed to Survey #3 to identify common barriers that were vital in the overall failure to achieve sustained improvements. Survey #3 consists of one question as follows:

If sustainment of, or improvements have not been gained from implementing Lean Manufacturing and/or Six Sigma select the top four barriers applicable.

- *Building a diverse work force*
- *Institutionalized expectations, values, and methods in the culture*
- *Development of a learning organization*
- *Ability to extend change to all areas of the organization*
- *Establishing leadership at the grass roots*
- *Gain short term wins during implementation*
- *Leadership that promotes a high level of loyalty*
- *Ability to align the vision with strategy*
- *Leadership that reduces levels of job stress and tension*

- *Empowering others for action*

- *Leadership that takes charge*

- *Excellent communications*

- *Create policies and procedures that support change*

- *Creating a vision*

- *Leadership that is well connected within the business*

- *Establishing a urgency for change*

Of the nine participants who preceded to Survey #3 the follow responses reflect the top three barriers to successful implementation of the operations excellence initiative.

Barrier	Count	Percentage
Establishing a urgency for change	9	23.08%
Creating a vision	8	20.51%
Excellent communications	6	15.38%
Ability to align the vision with strategy	6	15.38%
Institutionalizes expectations, values, and methods in the culture	6	15.38%

TABLE 3 Barriers to Implementation

Of the nine participants the highest percentage (23.08%) cite
establish a sense of urgency as the number one barrier leading to
their failed attempt. Secondly, 20.51% cited that *establishing a vision*
was the chief element lacking in the implementation effort. Finally, for
the number three barrier, respondents were split between three

elements each gaining 15.38% of the total answers; *excellent communications, ability to align vision to strategy, and institutionalize expectations, values and methods in the culture.*

Survey #4

Consisted of fifteen questions each providing an element critical to change leadership and the successful implementation of an operations excellence transformation for an organization. The same set of fifteen questions was given to two sets of participants. Each of the fifteen questions had the same potential responses as follows:

- *Not established*
- *Initial steps*
- *Somewhat established*
- *Established*
- *Institutionalized*

The intent of the survey is to establish the perceived level of successful achievement of the identified element in the operations excellence transformation; how well is leadership executing the change element. The first group was comprised on senior executives down to plant manager level within the business. The second group of participants being comprised of mid level managers down through individuals within the workforce. The management survey was sent to a total of 70 of which 46 responded. The workforce survey was sent to a total of 70 of which 61 responded.

From all respondents the following (Table 4) comprises the individual answers by percentage.

Barrier	Percentage
Not established	28%
Initial steps	25%
Somewhat established	21%
Established	22%
Institutionalized	5%

TABLE 4 Management & Workforce Responses

However, from the data collected via Advanced Survey database reflected that four participants failed to complete the survey, so these four surveys were removed from the total population to normalize the total responses. This data is provided in Table 5 below.

Barrier	Percentage
Not established	28%
Initial steps	25%
Somewhat established	21%
Established	21%
Institutionalized	5%

TABLE 5 Normalized Management & Workforce Responses

Normalization disrupted the overall outcomes by only 1%.

After data normalization the task was to break the data out into the two separate groups consisting of management and workforce respondents. Table 6 provides the breakdown of management responses overall.

Barrier	Percentage
Not established	12%
Initial steps	14%
Somewhat established	32%
Established	35%
Institutionalized	7%

TABLE 6 Management Subgroup Responses

Table 7 provides the breakdown of workforce responses

overall.

Barrier	Percentage
Not established	40%
Initial steps	34%
Somewhat established	12%
Established	11%
Institutionalized	3%

TABLE 7 Workforce Subgroup Responses

Comparison of both sets of overall responses indicates that the perceived success level of change leadership is bi-modal between the senior management members and those of the workforce. This separation between the two groups is a vital indicator of disparity in the overall success rate of implementation. Senior level managers have indicated that they are leading and driving implementation of operations excellence transformation to a minimum of "Somewhat Established" level to that of complete institutionalized within the culture. While the workforce on the other had has strongly indicated that overall implementation is not established or at best in the very initial steps.

Validity of Data

The use of on-line web based survey services offered through Advanced Survey (www.advancedsurvey.com) provides an independent clearing house for data collection and storage. Upon completion and publishing of the survey by the author, the survey content, structure, and data collected were secured and can not be altered even by the author. This includes a warning that is issued during the publishing phase of the survey creation that clearly identifies that once published, the survey can not be altered in order to maintain validity.

Participants were sent an invitation to participate in the survey which contains the web link to the site, as well as the log in survey number. Participants at their leisure could sign in to the particular survey of choice, complete the questions, the session was then closed out and the answers provided were logged into the database and compiled.

Advanced Survey compiles data such as:

- Number of participants completing the survey.
- Graphic display of the data.

- Breakdown per questions reflecting the count and percentage answered for each individual choices per each question.

Access to results data is via password log in by the author. The author then had ability to review the summary reports on-line or print to hard copy for file. Data collected and compiled within the database could not be altered or modified by the author.

Originality and Limitations

The surveys and data collected in response are original work conducted solely as research within this dissertation. No other individual, group, or association has had access to the data for modification, review, or development.

Limitations included the aspect that within the design of the survey and solicitation of participants, anonymity was lost preventing sub grouping of responses by industry/service sectors.

Summary

Research conducted during this study relied upon survey data as well as historical and actual case study information. The intent was to determine the level of successful implementation of operations excellence, identification of any constraints or barriers to implementation, and the establishment of change leadership roles that are critical to deployment.

The data gathering method made use of the services provided by Advanced Survey (www.advancedsurvey.com). Services provided include the creation, formatting, and posting of surveys via internet access. Data collection and correlation was provided as a service with basic statistical percentages captured per question answer with graphical display. Furthermore, Advanced Survey provides independent data storage and validity through publishing criteria that protect surveys from modification or data alteration.

The data base of the study included fifty participants representing industry and services. The groups will be sub divided to provide representation of major industrial and services sectors. Industry included pharmaceutical, telecommunications, consumer goods, and automotive, while services included health care, banking and insurance businesses.

CHAPTER 5: SUMMARY, RECOMMENDATIONS AND CONCLUSIONS

Summary

Current business and strategic models attempt to drive successful implementation of operations excellence through a project approach focused upon only the specific techniques that yield rapid high impact results but fail to be developed and matured into distinctive competencies required for sustained competitive advantage. The achievement of distinctive competencies will be rooted in the development and maturity of organizational structures, processes, and culture that has been lacking in a majority of previous transformation attempts leading to the high level of failure. Operations excellence therefore must be an organization transformation initiative in which change leadership roles are a crucial set of characteristics of overall success.

Based upon the research included, root cause of initiative failure in a traditionally managed organization stems from the fundamental lack of change leadership. Lack of a clear understanding that implementation of sustainable operations excellence is not simply about deploying techniques of lean manufacturing, but about the creation of distinctive competencies in the business resources. Resource capabilities built upon knowledge, establishment of new values, expectations, behaviors and standards of performance, as well as alignment of the organizational structure coupled with process improvement to support the new strategy. The true bottom line realization is that sustainable competitive advantage through operations excellence is only achievable through organizational transformation.

Research conducted as part of this study provided findings that support the original hypothesis regarding the failure of sustainable implementation of operations excellence stemming from three areas of importance:

- Identification of barriers common to the implementation of operations excellence.
- Reliance upon traditional models of development and implementation that focus only upon technical solutions and techniques versus an integrated model that combines techniques with change leadership.

- A disparity exists between perceived achievement of specific change leadership elements by management and workforce.

The combination of complacency, defensive behavior, routines, and inward focus are the enemy of progress; ultimately it creates a situation in which major change is needed within the business organization to stay competitive. In traditionally ran companies this change for survival typically manifest itself through strategic plans that include some level of operations excellence. Many companies embark upon this strategy based upon lean manufacturing programs with the intent of rapid high impact results in productivity and profitability.

Many of today's managers are well versed in the definitions of lean manufacturing methods and approaches. Yet, despite this familiarity, comparatively few organizations are implementing operations excellence successfully. Appendix B, Figure #25 contains the results of questions identifying the level of maturity and sustainability of implementation. The difficulty most managers have lies somewhere in the enormous gap between the technical details and the understanding of "how" to achieve it. Few traditional managers possess more than a vague idea of the specific day to day change leadership activities that are required to create and sustain an operations excellence culture at any level. Without this knowledge, efforts to establish the desired organization culture and required transformation are always marked with frustration, unfulfilled expectations, and loss of market share and profits.

Yet traditional management's obsession with fast results constrains the approach taken in the strategy. Fixation with technical solutions to issues leads to the selection and specific application of only techniques of lean manufacturing. The traditional hierarchy approach looks to develops solutions from higher levels within the organization then simply hands these actions down the chain of command as mandates for cost reductions. However, top management typically is out of touch with the weaknesses of the business or emerging threats that frontline employees understand through daily experience on the factory floor or in the face to face dealings with customers.

Such top driven change creates people problems; people resist having solutions imposed on them by individuals who lack intimate familiarity with their day to day operations. Their resistance is exposed through a lack of motivation and commitment to change. People follow work routines that are familiar, comfortable, safe, and satisfying, they are not eager to change unless given compelling reasons to do so. People also have social routines at work, associations with co-workers that satisfy their needs as humans and changes that impose on those routines are equally unwelcome. Traditional managers find that addressing straight forward technical issues are comparatively easy; ignoring the human side of change however is shortsighted and a symptom of ineffective management.

Top management often fails to understand why employees are not concerned about productivity, customer service, or cost. Too often this is because management has failed to put employees in touch with the relevant data. In the absence of that data, everything appears to be fine to the workforce. Change readiness as a condition of the organization is a state in which a high degree of motivation on the part of employees exists to change various aspects of the organization. This motivation typically is a result of substantial dissatisfaction with the status quo and an eagerness for something measurably better that creates a level of discomfort resulting in a clear sense of urgency. True sense of urgency must be present for real change to have a chance. Once the need for change has been expressed convincingly and broad support has been enlisted, that support must be maintained through a set of consistent behaviors and messages by management. Inconsistency in either will cause a damaging interpretation that management is either not serious about implementing change or unwilling to do its part.

Traditional implementation of operations excellence focuses upon the technical solutions thereby bypasses the vital elements of change leadership and organizational transformation, the "soft stuff" associated with change. In the rush to gain high impact results, traditional managers implement operations excellence in hope of performance increases or cost reductions that positively impact productivity or profit. Within a command and control hierarchy structure, the mandate is to cut cost typically leading to the roll out of a lean manufacturing program, but the entire application is that of single highly structured events with ready made solutions determined by management.

The failure of management through focusing on technical solutions and cost reductions while not addressing the soft human aspects associated with change creates barriers to implementation of operations excellence; which in its bare essence is an organizational transformation requiring both breakthrough and incremental improvements in culture as well as process. Appendix B, Figure #26 reflects the results by participants that identify common barriers to implementation of operations excellence.

In Survey #3 the highest percentage of responses identified the need of "establishing urgency for change". As a barrier, this one element can have significant impact on the implementation of

186

operations excellence. All employees from management through the entire workforce desire to understand why the change must occur, what the change will consist of, how will the change impact "my" job and their role in the organization? Without this understanding, there is a lack of ownership, buy in, and commitment. Traditional organizations bypass this essential element in the rush for results either in the belief that the employees will understand or do not have a need to know.

Survey #3 participants furthermore identified the lack of "creating a vision" as the number two barrier while "excellent communications", "ability to align the vision with strategy", and "institutionalize expectations, values, and methods in the culture" each tied as the number three response as an important barrier to successful execution. Each of these barriers highlights how critical change leadership is in the development and execution of an operations excellence initiative. Traditionally managed organizations fail to foster the required change leadership necessary to change, develop, and mature a sustaining culture.

The rush to implement a technique to gain rapid results is a fixation in traditional management philosophy that fails to create sustainable culture changes. Any competitive advantage that might be gained from the technique is soon lost since no distinctive competency has been established within the resources. Operations excellence at its very core is a change initiative, one that requires complete organizational transformation on a system wide level so that lean manufacturing standards become the very culture of the business; transformation that affects each level and function of the organization through leaning, focus, alignment, and sustainment of changes.

Managers must go beyond the daily activities which focus upon efficiency and technical applications such as SMED or JIT by providing effective leadership concerning fundamental elements of change such as; behaviors, expectations, motivation, and norms for both groups and individuals who will be utilizing the new techniques. Too be effective, the specific tools of lean manufacturing must be established in a way that at the actionable level of individuals and teams the change creates the desired expectations, fosters the new behaviors, and rewards enhanced performance. The application of both in a manner that creates an environment of learning, adaptation, new behaviors and beliefs coupled with enhanced skills provides an organization that deploys resources that are capable, flexible, and reliable; resources with distinctive competencies. These intangible elements can not be copied by competitors and therefore become the true essence of sustainable competitive advantage.

Meanwhile, many executives believe that their operations excellence implementations are moving ahead smoothly. Surveys of both management and workforce groups from various industries as to their perceptions about how well their organizations are dealing with common barriers of implementation and vital change leadership elements provide just cause for concern. The results are shown in Appendix B, Figure 5 through Figure 23.

It is clear that executives, in general, think they are doing a satisfactory job of leading their organizations toward operations excellence. In light of the workforces' ratings, executives appear to be overly optimistic in their assessments. There is little or no overlap between the ratings of non-management workers and those of executives, which is alarming. These results are even more astonishing when considering that many of the surveyed individuals were from organizations that claimed to be implementing lean manufacturing aggressively in their organizations.

The most important insight to be gained from the Survey #4, Appendix B Figure 27 is that the typical organization will continue to fail in its pursuit of operations excellence primarily because upper management believes that progress is being made. Believing that things are running smoothly, management will be slow to change or modify implementation strategies which in the short-term bleed away profit. Over the long-term, the complacency bred by this perception increases the odds that a competitor will implement an operations excellence culture more quickly and take away a large portion of the market.

The source of this problem can be found in the way management typically views processes and attempts to improve them. There are three basic categories in a process hierarchy. Going from least complex to most complex, the processes are described as micro, macro, and mega. Micro-processes are the work done by non-management personnel from hourly factory workers, to secretaries, and technicians. Soldering a joint and completing a purchase order are typical examples. Insofar as they provide the foundation for operations excellence, the behavior modification, process improvement, and measurement are fundamental to becoming world-class.

A macro-process is a name for a group of micro-processes. Product development is a macro-process, as are marketing, recruiting, accounts receivable, and so on. Macro-processes are easy to name and measure, but the measurements don't provide insights about the condition of specific component micro-processes. For example, knowing that shipments from a plant were 99.5 percent on-time for one week tells nothing about the health of the plant's micro-processes.

Mega-processes, such as an entire division, are agglomerations of many micro and macro-processes. Measurements of mega-processes such as profit, stock price, and so on are easy to track but provide absolutely no insight into the conditions of the macro and micro-processes that create mega-process results. As investors are all too aware, many organizations run into serious trouble just months after seeing record profits and stock price increases.

Executives and upper-level managers are expected to create favorable mega-process outputs for shareholders. One of the difficulties is that all mega-process outputs are time-delayed, averaged, distorted and homogenized results of thousands of micro-processes that occurred days, weeks and months earlier. By the time an executive sees a profit impact; the root causes have been operating for a long time. The traditional manager is working far behind the power curve of cause and effect when he or she reacts to quarterly results.

A second circumstance further complicates affairs for the traditional manager. Without change leadership to exert leverage on micro-processes, the traditional manager turns to the only weapon available: technology and in vogue techniques. The traditional manager is constantly seeking to hit a homerun with every bold, new idea, attempting to get a quick, large increase in some aspect of the organization's performance results. The problem is that most new technical solutions implemented are not self-sustaining. The result is that a traditional organization tries to solve every problem with new schemes which become perceived as the flavor of the month.

Of course, driven by shareholder demands, traditional managers do not see an alternative. Not fully understanding how to implement operations excellence these executives are driven to embrace each new concept that involves technology and large-scale, wide-ranging initiatives such as TQM, lean manufacturing, re-engineering, etc. In many cases, these actions are sound business decisions, but many are simply stabs in the dark. As the old saying goes, "if all you have is a hammer, pretty soon everything starts to look like a nail."

The worst issue with the application of techniques without change leadership is that they provide no significant, long-lasting competitive lead. At best, even if a technique works as planned, the only gain is a momentary lead that is quickly copied by the industry. At best the organization will be playing catch up with other businesses that have already started with the same idea, the lead always evaporates after a few years, as market dynamics change and different strengths and technologies become important.

A further complication is that the drive for cost reductions, higher quality, and reduced lead times make many of the buzz term concepts absolutely critical to survival and success. A management team that lives and dies on the latest industry concept or buzz cannot afford to pass one up, so it forces many ill-advised applications on the organization, while bypassing any attempts to fix faulty micro-processes and create sustaining transformation of the culture. This is not the road to world-class performance.

Recommendations

To achieve full successful implementation of operations excellence there must be an integrated model that incorporates both the hard technical tools of lean manufacturing with the vital aspects of change leadership and organizational transformation. Only through an integrated approach can full and lasting changes in values, expectations, behaviors and norms be modified to create and maintain resources with distinctive competencies. This combination of explicit and implicit capabilities provides the balance of competencies that others can not copy, hence a sustainable competitive advantage. This achievement requires, (Figure 4):

- Solid leadership that:
  - Communicates the vision.
  - Facilitates and models the behaviors of operations excellence.
  - Sets the standards for the organization.
  - Assists the workforce in adapting to the change.
  - Builds trust and inspires commitment.
  - Coaches and develops the workforce.
  - Constantly challenges the system.
- A team based culture that:
  - Focus on empowerment concepts.
  - Is structured upon self directed teams.
  - Leverage the knowledge of highly skilled workers.
  - Promotes employee accountability and responsibility.
  - Advocates the continual development of the workforce.
  - Values diversity.
  - Believes that employee ownership of the final product is shared throughout the process.
- A communication system that:

- o Utilizes both formal and informal communication means.
- o Advocates and fosters open communications in a fear free environment.
- o Encourages decision making at the lowest level appropriate.
- o Promotes knowledge sharing between hourly workers and management.
- o Drives the behaviors of internal operations, as well as focus on the behaviors of suppliers and customers.
- A simultaneous development processes that:
  - o Uses continuous improvement processes to identify the non-value added problems.
  - o Drives commitment to eliminating problems.
  - o Promotes constant improvement throughout the system.
  - o Leverages the knowledge of the organization with the knowledge bases of suppliers and customers.
  - o Continually trains and develops highly skilled workers.
  - o Uses scoreboards or measurement systems to monitor progress.

Appendix C, Figure 29 through 32, provides a traditional implementation model currently used within industry. This model consist of four phases; *Beginning, Improving, Succeeding, and Leading.* Each phase relies upon the sequential development and maturity of the previous phase. Yet, focus of activities within each phase relies only upon technical solutions and techniques.

Phase One as an example concentrates upon stability within the organization through the implementation of tools such as Root Cause Analysis, Inventory Control, Corrective Action Process, etc. No time or resources are dedicated in the traditional model to the development of understanding of what needs to change and why the change is required. Nor is there any effort to create a sense of urgency in the workforce as to why the organization must change. No vision of what the organization will look like in the future is provided and the use of extensive communication and leadership commitment are lacking. These are the very foundation so vital to understanding change and providing leadership required for organizational transformation to operations excellence.

Figure 33 through 36 provides a new operation excellence transformation model based upon this research that creates total integration of techniques of lean manufacturing with the critical organizational transformation elements so vital to leading and sustaining a strategic change initiative such as operations excellence. The four phases of this model consist of; *Learning, Focus, Alignment, and Sustaining.*

The learning phase creates the organizational understanding while the second phase establishes focused transformation through the prioritization on a few critical initiatives, detailed planning, deployment, and execution of micro level processes and behavior changes. Phase three, align, provides the structure to engage building teamwork, coaching by leadership, and organizational cross functional ownership within all support functions. Finally in phase four, sustain, a maturity in the culture has been created that institutionalizes operations excellence founded upon distinctive competencies embedded within the culture.

Specifically within phase one, the technical solutions of the traditional model are paired with the vital aspects of development of the business need for change, creating understanding of the change, how the change will impact the organization, and essential change leadership principles. Essentially, leadership must be creating a condition of change readiness; a high degree of motivation on the part of employees to change aspects of the organization. This motivation typically results from tangible dissatisfaction with the status quo and an eagerness for something measurably better. A certain level of nervousness, fear, or discomfort resulting in a clear sense of urgency must be in the air for real change to have a chance.

Change leaders raise concerns about current situations regarding productivity and profitability while traditional management often fails to understand why employees are not concerned about productivity, customer service, or cost. Too often this is because management has failed to put employees in touch with the relevant data. In the absence of that data, everything appears to be fine. Change leadership must create opportunities for employees to educate management about the dissatisfaction and problems they experience through open dialogue and the setting of high standards and expectations.

The starting point for any effective change efforts is a clear definition of the business problem. Problem identification answers the most important questions that affected personnel want to know. Why must we do this? How the problem is identified is also important; motivation and commitment to change are greatest when the people who will have to make the change and live with it are instrumental in identifying the problem and planning its solution. Assess current business conditions both internal and external to the company then develop the story line of why the business must change and how the change will affect individuals on a personal level.

The initiative leadership must be selected and assigned not only based on technical expertise but their persistent belief that transformation is key to competitiveness and a deep conviction that fundamental change will have a major impact on the bottom line. The change leaders must be able to articulate their conviction in the form of credible and compelling vision. People will not buy into the pain and effort of change unless they can see a future state that is tangibly better for them. Leadership must have the people skills and organizational know how to implement their vision while utilizing the soft skills to deal with the human side of operations excellence and the associated transformation of the culture to one of sustainable competitive advantage. The bottom line is that organizational change leaders must have a complete understanding of change leadership, organizational culture, and the methods required to modify both human and group behaviors and norms.

Phase one in the new model provides a spotlight on the development of commitment within leadership. This commitment comes through the establishment of leaders who desire to change the organization, have a deep understanding of the critical aspects of culture change leadership coupled with the clear expectation of cross functional support from all areas of the organization to execute. Meanwhile, this new model provides fundamental organizational structures to support operations excellence via platforms such as; plant steering team, champions, operations excellence leader, self directed teams, etc.

Throughout the entire model communications plays a crucial role as an effective tool for motivating and setting the tone for change. Several key elements of communication in the change leadership role include:

- Specify the nature of the change
- Explain why
- Explain the scope of change
- Develop a mental picture of change that is understood within the minds of the workforce.
- Predict negative aspects of implementation
- Explain the criteria for success and how it will be measured
- Explain how people will be rewarded for success
- Repeat, repeat, and repeat the purpose of change
- Use all medias of communication
- Make communication two way

Figure 34 represents phase two or the focus phase. Here the development of a shared vision reflecting the competitive future of the organization should clearly provide scope and a baseline common to all employees from senior executives to front line workers of how the business will be structured, conduct processes, and how to organize and manage for competitive position. Change leadership must develop a clear vision of an altered and improved future. They must also be able to communicate that vision to others in a way that makes the benefits of change clear. How the change will improve the business and how those improvements will benefit employees. An effective vision should:

- Describe a desirable future that people will be happy to have and create.
- Be compelling, so much better than the current state that they will gladly undertake the effort and sacrifice as necessary to attain it.
- Be realistic and within the grasp
- Be focused by limiting itself to manageable and coherent set of objectives and goals.
- Be flexible, to adapt to changing circumstances

- Be easy to communicate at all levels of the business including internal and external.

Organizational structuring began in phase one continues to develop through phase two with the deployment of resources based on the few critical initiatives with cross functional ownership by leadership and workforce at the micro levels. This integration of ownership ensures that support functions have been pulled into the plan development and action items establishing the ownership necessary for commitment and the desire for change. Policy deployment is the process utilized within this new model to establish organizational alignment and focus. This methodology provides focus through the development and prioritization of the few key initiatives that the organization leadership wishes to concentrate upon and utilize its scarce resources in the achievement of competitive advantage. Furthermore, policy deployment ensures alignment of objectives and goals to the limited resources supporting one another in their efforts and developing synergy of action.

During phase two, leadership development proceeds with increased defining of change leadership roles, responsibility, ownership, and authority of execution. Leadership participates in and receives a large amount of training on various business fundamentals, critical thinking, facilitation, as well as an immersion into organizational development and culture change. Training should concentrate upon the three key elements of; change, organizational culture and development, and leadership. In the drive to implement the operations excellence strategy the model must include a strong foundation of human dynamics and organizational environments.

Top leadership through all levels of the workforce must have an understanding of culture change, human behaviors, norms, and social criteria to facilitate operations excellence transformation of the business. Leadership is vital in this role as the change leaders and therefore the overall tone of execution will be based upon their ability to motivate others, create the desired environment supporting the need and sense of urgency to change, as well as the defining and exemplification of desired behaviors. Imperative within the operations excellence transformation, leadership must continue the relentless communication via both formal and informal methods. This process should utilize all available medias with open and frank dialogue horizontally and vertically within the organization.

Meanwhile, policies to support and facilitate change must be created or existing ones redefined to ensure that decision making is consistent with the vision, strategy, and operations while at the same time allowing considerable latitude to employees for empowerment.

Polices are directives designed to guide the thinking, decisions, and actions of managers and their subordinates in implementing the businesses strategy increasing effectiveness by standardizing many routine decisions and clarifying the discretion leadership and subordinates can exercise in implementing functional actions. Furthermore, polices establish indirect control over independent action, promote uniform handling of similar activities, ensure quicker decisions through standardization and institutionalizing basic aspects of organizational behavior reducing uncertainty in repetitive and day to day decision making.

A key element often over looked in the rush to attain rapid results is the creation of a detailed implementation plan. Once the few key initiatives have been decided upon the detail action steps requiring execution must be identified, assigned ownership, resources, a specific timeline for accomplishment, and a metric to gage progress. The plan should contain enough detail to provide full scope of actions as well as understanding of criteria and expectations of achievement. This plan must be communicated to all levels of the organization to ensure understanding as well as the establishment of commitment to execution.

The crucial element in phase two for change leadership hinges on the forming and deployment of teams based upon natural work groups and micro process level ownership. These teams concentrate on the execution of new process techniques while leadership provides the mentoring of new desired behaviors and standard procedures. Each of these structured engagements and teams are directly linked via measurable performance goals integral to the overall strategy of operations excellence and the attainment of the vision.

Phase three, align allows the roll out of changes to extend to other units without pushing it from the top. The likelihood of success is greatest when change is instigated in small, fairly autonomous units. Changing an entire organization at once is much more difficult and less likely to succeed. Once change on a small scale is accomplished and witnessed by employees in adjacent units, diffusion of the change initiative throughout the organization is much more likely.

Empowered teams have been given timely and appropriate training that builds critical thinking, business understanding, and empowerment to engage in a fear free environment designed to foster learning and adaptation. Leadership continues to coach individuals and teams while communicating the expectations and providing progress reviews in relation to the overall implementation plan.

Leadership is engaged through active execution but more importantly visible to the entire organization as an example of desired behaviors, values, and norms.

As the performance gains are made and the new behaviors become standardized they mature into the new norms within the organization to institutionalize success through systems, structures, and controls. Gains can be consolidated and cemented through policies that describe how work is to be done, through information systems and through new reporting relationships.

By this time in the model, phase four, sustaining, the organizational resources have deployed and executed specific techniques as well as institutionalized the transformed culture within the organization. The operations excellence system has become the culture and therefore has established sustainability. These new breakthrough and continuous performance enhancements have established distinctive competencies within the company resources, thereby creating a sustainable competitive advantage.

Self directed work teams are in place and fully functional driving process improvements and adaptation to a point of directing and sustaining themselves in the change process, application of operations excellence techniques, and daily management aspects.

Communications at this point closes the circle of improvement by providing vital feedback integration and assessment to complete the cycle of improvement. This bridge is vital to the overall operations excellence model by closing the gap of performance enhancement and outcomes with input back on the changes that have been put into affect, impact of positive and negative outcomes, and learning through after action reports. Assessments permit independent verification of the maturity level attained as well as the ability to sustain the changes.

Conclusion

The study contradicts previous research in that much of the existing documentation is skewed for only technical aspects and benefits of implementing lean manufacturing. This is exemplified by the consulting firms, publishing houses and authors, countless seminars and courses that have followed suite catering to businesses seeking expertise and have locked on to the traditional aspects of operations excellence in a hope of achieving rapid high impact results in performance. All look to capitalize upon the desires of businesses for performance enhancement, a condition that has been perpetuated by the heightened appeal of operations excellence. Yet, for all of their expertise, these single focused events based upon the technical solutions conform to traditional management practices without any detail of how to accomplish sustainable competitive advantage with operations excellence.

Mr. Womack has written several best selling books presenting on a high level the benefits of lean and lean manufacturing for businesses. Each expands on the reasons why lean is important and why lean should be implemented coupled with the overall benefits of implementation. Yet, Mr. Womack fails to provide the most important step in implementation of lean, the vital soft stuff concerning human resources and the creation of distinctive competencies that create sustainable competitive advantage through transformation of the organizational culture.

This reinforces the concept of traditional management that to successfully implement operations excellence there is only a need to deploy specific selected tools such as JIT, SMED, TPM, etc. in areas of the business needing some level of cost reductions or performance improvements. Only the technical aspects of lean manufacturing are expanded upon, no change leadership or organizational culture aspects are addressed; the foundation to establishing a transformed culture that is capable of sustaining competitive advantage.

This study has attempted to examine current industrial and business initiatives and their drive to apply operations excellence concepts of lean manufacturing. The study identified common barriers to successful deployment of operations excellence which stem from the traditional management failure to execute operations excellence as a change initiative and simply as an event to gain rapid results.

Due to the limited nature of research on operations excellence transformation available as a strategy for sustainable competitive advantage it is recommended that further independent studies be conducted to expand upon and elaborate on the aspects of change leadership, organizational transformation, culture, and sustainable competitive advantage of operations excellence.

The alternative to the traditional model is a new integrated model for operations excellence transformation that combines the application of the various techniques of lean manufacturing with the organizational culture change elements necessary to develop resources capable of sustaining results. A transformation that is system wide and encompasses the organization. Not properly handled, operations excellence implementations typically fade away as failed "programs of the month."

Any individual micro-process improvement in a lean system is like a snowflake. Taken one at a time, each is almost nothing. But, when enough of them are piled together, continuously without pause, they create a massive glacier that cannot be stopped. That is what operations excellence is, a competitive culture built upon thousands of improvements that cannot be dismissed. These micro-process improvement behaviors amount to the primary difference between world-class and traditional organizations.

Anyone can buy a technological based concept, but it is impossible to buy an operations excellence culture. Each lean manufacturing implementation must be developed on-site, adapted by the people to mesh with all the "nooks and crannies" of the organization. While the basic principles of lean are the same in any organization, each implementation is unique. This is why successful operations excellence organizations are always very open about hosting tours and telling everyone, including competitors how they did it. They know that the "lean tourists" are looking for a technological solution, a quick and easy way to improve their organization. There isn't one.

BIBLIOGRAPHY

Allen, J., Robinson, C., & Stewart, D. (2001). *Lean Manufacturing: A Plant Floor Guide.* Detroit, MI: Society of Manufacturing Engineers.

Anderson, L. A., & Anderson, D. (2001). *The Change Leader's Roadmap: How To Navigate Your Organization's Transformation.* San Francisco, CA: Jossey-Bass/Pfeiffer.

Bossidy, L., & Charan, R. (2002). *Execution: The Discipline of Getting Things Done.* New York: Crown Publishing Group.

Cowley, M., & Domb, E. (1997). *Beyond Strategic Vision: Effective Corporate Action with Hoshin Planning.* Boston: Butterworth-Heinemann.

Draft, R. L. (2001). *Organization Theory and Design.* Cincinnati, Ohio: South-Western College Publishing.

Feld, W. M. (2001). *Lean Manufacturing: Tools, Techniques, and How To Use Them.* Boca Raton, FL: St. Lucie Press.

Fogg, C. D. (1999). *Implementing Your Strategic Plan: How to Turn "Intent" Into Effective Action for Sustainable Change.* New

York: American Management Association Publications.

George, M. L. (2002). *Lean Six Sigma: Combining Six Sigma Quality with Lean Speed.* New York: McGraw-Hill.

Hamel, G., & Prahalad, C.K. (1994). *Competing for the Future: Breakthrough Strategies for Seizing Control of your Industry and Creating the Markets of Tomorrow.* Boston: Harvard Business School Press.

Kaplan, R. S., & Norton, D. P. (2001). *The Strategy Focused Organization: How Balanced Scorecard Companies Thrive in the New Business Environment.* Boston: Harvard Business School Press.

Kotter, J. P. (1996). *Leading Change.* Boston: Harvard Business School Press.

Lareau, E. W. (2000). *Lean Leadership: From Chaos to Carrots to Commitment.* Davenport, IA: Midland Press Corporation.

Pearce, J. A., & Robinson, R. B. (2003). *Strategic Management: Formulation, Implementation and Control.* Boston: McGraw-Hill Irwin.

Peters, T. (1997). *The Circle of Innovation: You Can't Shrink Your Way to Greatness.* New York: Alfred A. Knopf, Inc.

Pietersen, W. G. (2002). *Reinventing Strategy: Using Strategic Learning to Create & Sustain Breakthrough Performance.* New York: John Wiley & Sons, Inc.

Phillips, D. T. (1997). The *Founding Fathers on Leadership: Classic Teamwork in Changing Times.* New York: Warner Books, Inc.

Phillips, D. T. (1992). *Lincoln on Leadership: Executive Strategies "For Tough Times."* New York: Warner Books, Inc.

Porter, M. E. (1985). *Competitive Advantage: Creating and Sustaining Superior Performance.* New York: The Free Press.

Sullivan, G. R., & Harper, M. V. (1996). *Hope is not a Method: What Business Leaders Can Learn from America's Army.* NY: Broadway Books.

Womack, J. P., & Jones, D. T. (1996). *Lean Thinking: Banish Waste and Create Wealth in your Corporation.* New York: Simon & Schuster.

APPENDICES

APPENDIX A

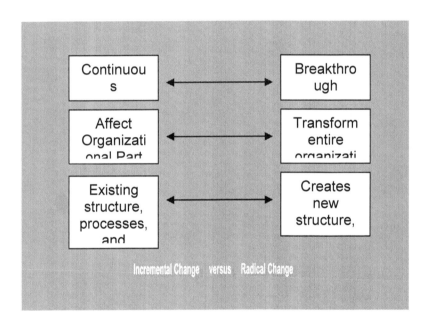

FIGURE 1

Cowley and Domb, (1997). *Beyond Strategic Vision: Effective Corporate Action with Hoshin Planning.* P.18

"The hard stuff is easy, the soft stuff is hard."

If you understood 100% of all of the technical aspects of Lean, you would only be 50% of the way there.

FIGURE 2

Ingersoll Rand, (2002). *Change Management During Implementation.*

Slide 7

The absence
of a major crisis

Too many
visible resources

Too much happy talk
From senior management

Complacency

Low overall
Performance
Standards

Human nature, with its
Capacity for denial,
Especially if people are
Already busy and stressed

Organizational structures
that focuses
Employees on narrow
Functional goals

A kill-the-messenger-of-bad-news,
Low candor, low-confrontation culture

A lack of sufficient
Performance feedback
From external sources

Internal measurement
Systems that focus on the
Wrong performance indexes

FIGURE 3

Casey, (2005). *The Role of Change Leadership*
In A
Operations Excellence Transformation Model. P.161

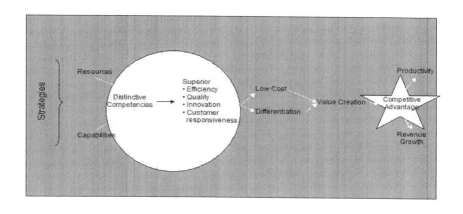

FIGURE 4

Casey, (2005). *The Role of Change Leadership*

In A

Operations Excellence Transformation Model. P.162

APPENDIX B

Percentage

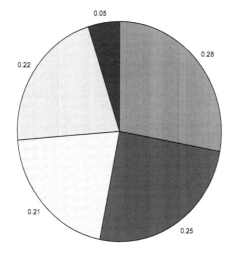

0.05

0.28

0.22

0.21

0.25

Not Established
Initial Steps
Somewhat Established
Established
Institutionalized

FIGURE 5
Overall Results by Response

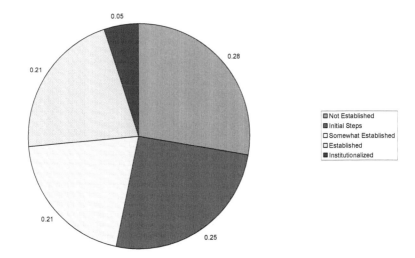

FIGURE 6

Normalized Overall Results by Response with Non Completed surveys removed

Management

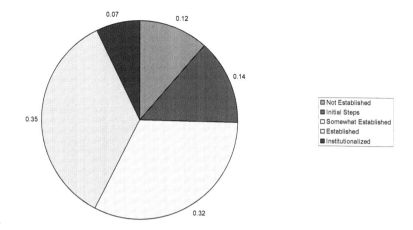

FIGURE 7
Overall Results for Management

Workforce pie

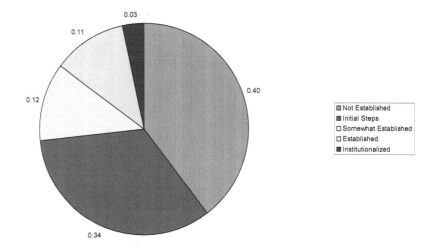

FIGURE 8
Overall Results for Workforce

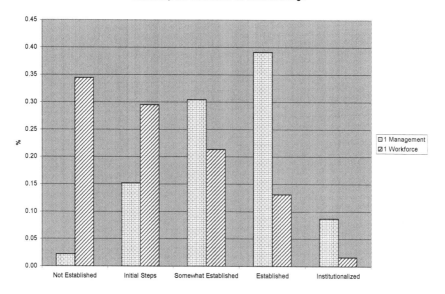

Leadership has established the need for change

FIGURE 9

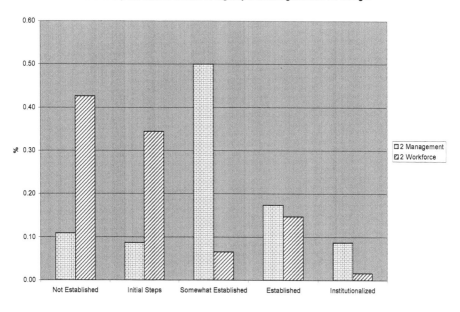

Leadership has created a sense of urgency concerning the need for change.

FIGURE 10

Leadership has a cledar vision for operations excellence.

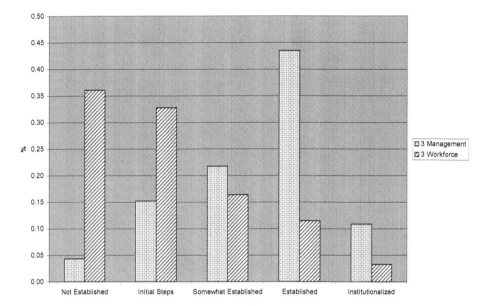

FIGURE 11

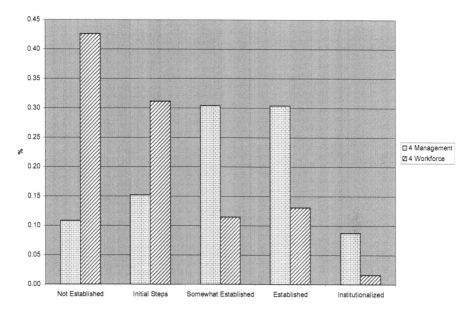

FIGURE 12

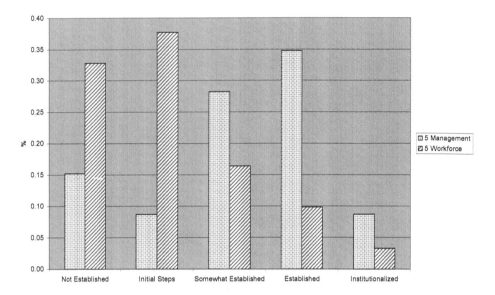

A cross functional leadership team has been created to act as the guiding force for operations excellence.

FIGURE 13

Leadership has ensured strategic initiatives are prioritized, focused and cross functionally owned.

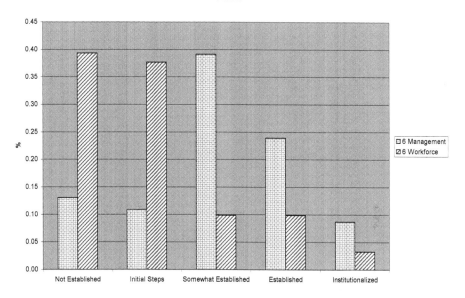

FIGURE 14

Leadership guides actions to achieve short term wins to build commitment.

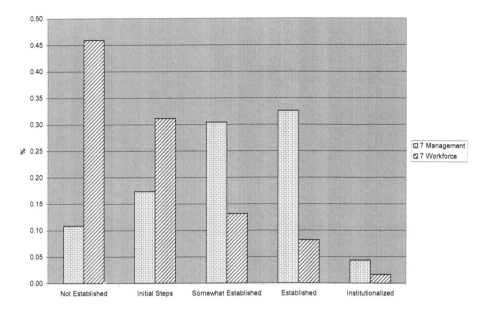

FIGURE 15

Desired expectations and outcomes are reinforced and rewarded by leadership.

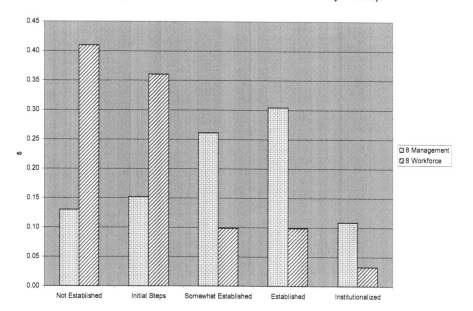

FIGURE 16

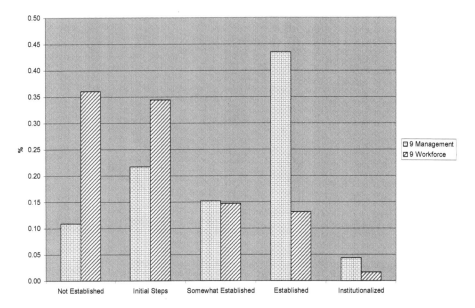

FIGURE 17

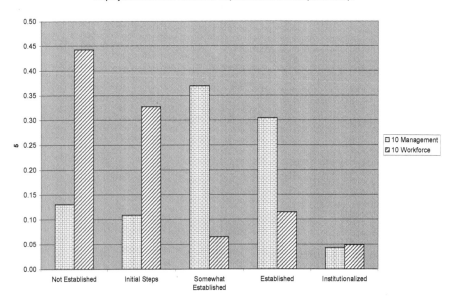

FIGURE 18

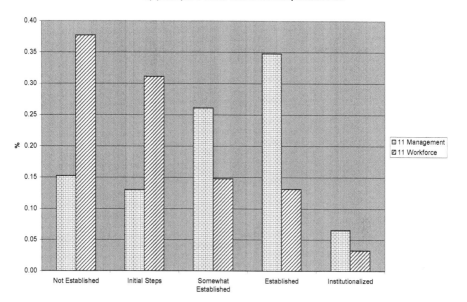

FIGURE 19

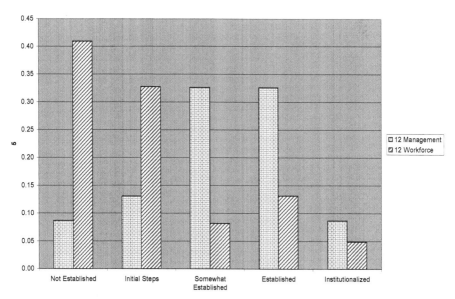

FIGURE 20

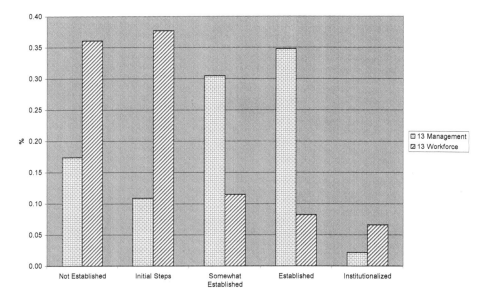

Leadership has driven the operations excellence change to include suppliers and customers.

FIGURE 21

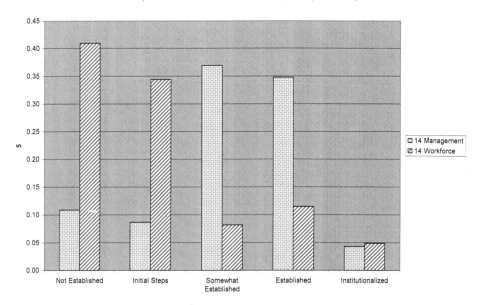

New expectations and behaviors are exemplified by leadership.

FIGURE 22

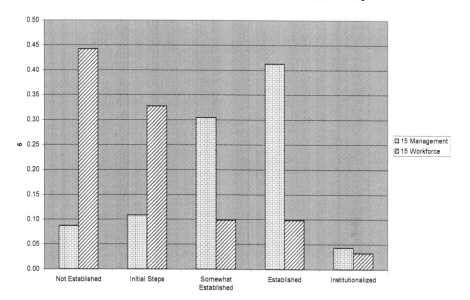

FIGURE 23

Advanced Survey

| My Account | Surveys | Questions | Participants | **Results** |

Survey Results #1

Below are the real-time results for your survey. Select a question to filter the results.

Selected Survey: Grand Strategies

Survey Question/Answers	Count	Percent	Graph
1. From the list below of grand strategies identify the one (1) initiative that your company has placed emphasis upon as its priority.			
Product innovation	2	5.88%	
Market growth	8	23.53%	
Greater customer service	5	14.71%	
Lean Manufacturing	9	26.47%	
Acquisition/Divesting	0	0.00%	
Supply Chain Management/Partnerships	2	5.88%	
Six Sigma	7	20.59%	
Share technology	1	2.94%	
Total Quality Management	0	0.00%	

Total Survey Participants Answering At Least One Question ?: 34

Upgrade To An Enhanced Account For Greater Flexibility

- Download survey results in multiple formats
- Remove the Advanced Survey logo-bar from your surveys
- Specify an exact date for your survey to close
- Prevent users from taking a survey more than once

Full Benefits List | Upgrade Now »

Ask A Question | Make A Suggestion | Report A Problem
About Us | Account Types | Account Pricing | Your Privacy | User Agreement | Help

/results/results.asp - 69.2.211.203

http://www.advancedsurvey.com/results/results.asp

FIGURE 24

Survey Results

Below are the real-time results for your survey. Select a question to filter the results.

Selected Survey: Sustainment ☑

Survey Question/Answers	Count	Percent	Graph
1. Implementation of the Lean Manufacturing and/or Six Sigma initiative has reached what level of developmental maturity in the organization:			
Sustaining results after 12 months	0	0.00%	
Sustaining results for less than 12 months	2	16.67%	
Not sustaining results	6	50.00%	
No improvement results gained	3	25.00%	
Did not complete the implementation	1	8.33%	

Total Survey Participants Answering At Least One Question ?: 12

Upgrade To An Enhanced Account For Greater Flexibility

- Download survey results in multiple formats
- Remove the Advanced Survey logo-bar from your surveys
- Specify an exact date for your survey to close
- Prevent users from taking a survey more than once

Full Benefits List | Upgrade Now »

Ask A Question | Make A Suggestion | Report A Problem
About Us | Account Types | Account Pricing | Your Privacy | User Agreement | Help

/results/results.asp - 89.2.211.203

http://www.advancedsurvey.com/results/results.asp

FIGURE 25

Advanced**Survey**

| My Account | Surveys | Questions | Participants | **Results** |

Survey Results

Below are the real-time results for your survey. Select a question to filter the results.

Selected Survey: Top four

Survey Question/Answers	Count	Percent	Graph
1. If sustainment of, or improvements have not been gained from implementing Lean Manufacturing or Six Sigma select the top four barriers applicable			
Building a diverse work force	0	0.00%	
Institutionalizes expectations, values, and methods in the culture	6	15.38%	
Development of a learning organization	0	0.00%	
Ability to extend change to all areas of the organization	2	5.13%	
Establishing leadership at the grass roots	0	0.00%	
Gain short term wins during implementation	0	0.00%	
Leadership that promotes a high level of loyalty	0	0.00%	
Ability to align the vision with strategy	6	15.38%	
Leadership that reduces levels of job stress and tension	0	0.00%	
Empowering others for action	2	5.13%	
Leadership that takes charge	0	0.00%	
Excellent communications	6	15.38%	
Create policies and procedures that support change	0	0.00%	
Creating a vision	8	20.51%	
Leadership that is well connected within the business	0	0.00%	
Establishing a urgency for change	9	23.08%	

Total Survey Participants Answering At Least One Question ?: 10

Upgrade To An Enhanced Account For Greater Flexibility

- Download survey results in multiple formats
- Remove the Advanced Survey logo-bar from your surveys
- Specify an exact date for your survey to close
- Prevent users from taking a survey more than once

FIGURE 26

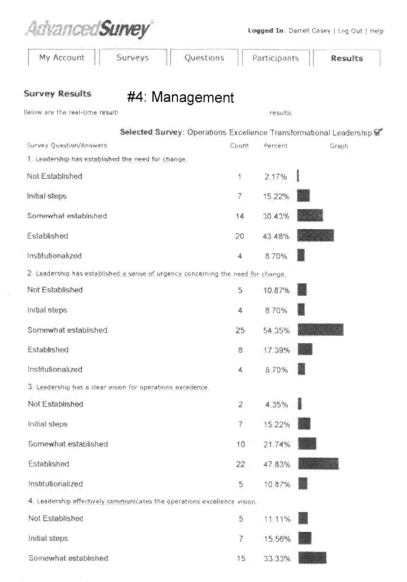

http://www.advancedsurvey.com/results/results.asp

FIGURE 27

241

Established	14	31.11%
Institutionalized	4	8.89%

5. A cross functional leadership team has been created to act as the guiding force for operations excellence change.

Not Established	7	15.56%
Initial steps	4	8.89%
Somewhat established	13	28.89%
Established	17	37.78%
Institutionalized	4	8.89%

6. Leadership has ensured strategic initiatives are prioritized, focused and cross functionally owned.

Not Established	6	13.64%
Initial steps	5	11.36%
Somewhat established	18	40.91%
Established	11	25.00%
Institutionalized	4	9.09%

7. Leadership guides actions to achieve short term wins to build commitment.

Not Established	5	11.36%
Initial steps	8	18.18%
Somewhat established	14	31.82%
Established	15	34.09%
Institutionalized	2	4.55%

8. Desired expectations and outcomes are re-enforced and rewarded by leadership.

Not Established	6	13.64%
Initial steps	7	15.91%
Somewhat established	12	27.27%
Established	14	31.82%
Institutionalized	5	11.36%

9. Leadership effectively removes implementation obstacles.

Not Established	5	11.36%
Initial steps	10	22.73%

FIGURE 27

Somewhat established	7	15.91%	
Established	20	45.45%	
Institutionalized	2	4.55%	

10. Employees and teams have been empowered for action by leadership.

Not Established	6	13.64%	
Initial steps	5	11.36%	
Somewhat established	17	38.64%	
Established	14	31.82%	
Institutionalized	2	4.55%	

11. Leadership participates in and shares ownership in activities.

Not Established	7	15.91%	
Initial steps	6	13.64%	
Somewhat established	12	27.27%	
Established	16	36.36%	
Institutionalized	3	6.82%	

12. Leadership provides emphasis on training and development of new skills.

Not Established	4	9.09%	
Initial steps	6	13.64%	
Somewhat established	15	34.09%	
Established	15	34.09%	
Institutionalized	4	9.09%	

13. Leadership has driven the operations excellence change to include suppliers and customers.

Not Established	8	18.18%	
Initial steps	5	11.36%	
Somewhat established	14	31.82%	
Established	16	36.36%	
Institutionalized	1	2.27%	

14. New expectations and behaviors are exemplified by leadership.

| Not Established | 5 | 11.36% | |

FIGURE 27

Initial steps	4	9.09%	
Somewhat established	17	38.64%	
Established	16	36.36%	
Institutionalized	2	4.55%	

15. Leadership provides focus and structure to ensure sustainment of change.

Not Established	4	9.09%	
Initial steps	5	11.36%	
Somewhat established	14	31.82%	
Established	19	43.18%	
Institutionalized	2	4.55%	

Total Survey Participants Answering At Least One Question ?: 46

Upgrade To An Enhanced Account For Greater Flexibility

- Download survey results in multiple formats
- Remove the Advanced Survey logo-bar from your surveys
- Specify an exact date for your survey to close
- Prevent users from taking a survey more than once

Full Benefits List | Upgrade Now »

Ask A Question | Make A Suggestion | Report A Problem
About Us | Account Types | Account Pricing | Your Privacy | User Agreement | Help

Copyright © 1999-2004 Advanced Survey. All rights reserved.

/results/results.asp - 69.2.211.203

http://www.advancedsurvey.com/results/results.asp

FIGURE 27

FIGURE 28

Established	8	13.11%
Institutionalized	1	1.64%

5. A cross functional leadership team has been created to act as the guiding force for operations excellence change.

Not Established	20	32.79%
Initial steps	23	37.70%
Somewhat established	10	16.39%
Established	6	9.84%
Institutionalized	2	3.28%

6. Leadership has ensured strategic initiatives are prioritized, focused and cross functionally owned.

Not Established	24	39.34%
Initial steps	23	37.70%
Somewhat established	6	9.84%
Established	6	9.84%
Institutionalized	2	3.28%

7. Leadership guides actions to achieve short term wins to build commitment.

Not Established	28	45.90%
Initial steps	19	31.15%
Somewhat established	8	13.11%
Established	5	8.20%
Institutionalized	1	1.64%

8. Desired expectations and outcomes are re-enforced and rewarded by leadership.

Not Established	25	40.98%
Initial steps	22	36.07%
Somewhat established	6	9.84%
Established	6	9.84%
Institutionalized	2	3.28%

9. Leadership effectively removes implementation obstacles.

Not Established	22	36.07%
Initial steps	21	34.43%

http://www.advancedsurvey.com/results/results.asp

FIGURE 28

Somewhat established	9	14.75%	
Established	8	13.11%	
Institutionalized	1	1.64%	

10. Employees and teams have been empowered for action by leadership.

Not Established	27	44.26%	
Initial steps	20	32.79%	
Somewhat established	4	6.56%	
Established	7	11.48%	
Institutionalized	3	4.92%	

11. Leadership participates in and shares ownership in activities.

Not Established	23	37.70%	
Initial steps	19	31.15%	
Somewhat established	9	14.75%	
Established	8	13.11%	
Institutionalized	2	3.28%	

12. Leadership provides emphasis on training and development of new skills.

Not Established	25	40.98%	
Initial steps	20	32.79%	
Somewhat established	5	8.20%	
Established	8	13.11%	
Institutionalized	3	4.92%	

13. Leadership has driven the operations excellence change to include suppliers and customers.

Not Established	22	36.07%	
Initial steps	23	37.70%	
Somewhat established	7	11.48%	
Established	5	8.20%	
Institutionalized	4	6.56%	

14. New expectations and behaviors are exemplified by leadership.

| Not Established | 25 | 40.98% | |

FIGURE 28

Initial steps	21	34.43%	
Somewhat established	5	8.20%	
Established	7	11.48%	
Institutionalized	3	4.92%	

15. Leadership provides focus and structure to ensure sustainment of change.

Not Established	27	44.26%	
Initial steps	20	32.79%	
Somewhat established	6	9.84%	
Established	6	9.84%	
Institutionalized	2	3.28%	

Total Survey Participants Answering At Least One Question ?: 61

Upgrade To An Enhanced Account For Greater Flexibility

- Download survey results in multiple formats
- Remove the Advanced Survey logo-bar from your surveys
- Specify an exact date for your survey to close
- Prevent users from taking a survey more than once

Full Benefits List | Upgrade Now »

Ask A Question | Make A Suggestion | Report A Problem
About Us | Account Types | Account Pricing | Your Privacy | User Agreement | Help

/results/results.asp - 69.2.211.203

http://www.advancedsurvey.com/results/results.asp

FIGURE 28

APPENDIX C

Phase 1: Beainnina (Stability)

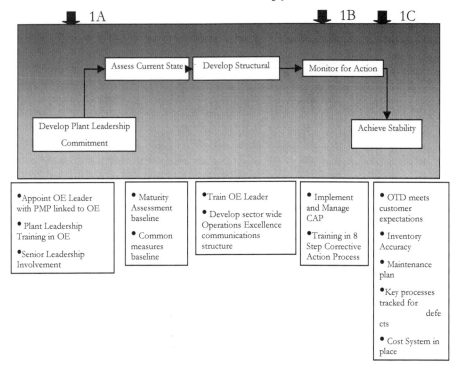

FIGURE 29

**Phase One - Traditional Operations Excellence Implementation
Model**

Phase 2: Improving (Continuous

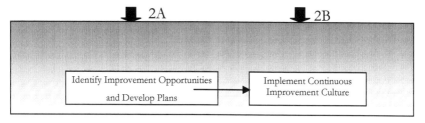

2A   **2B**

| Identify Improvement Opportunities and Develop Plans | → | Implement Continuous Improvement Culture |

- Create VSM - Order fulfillment
    - Current
    - Future
    - Ideal
- 7 Types of Waste
- Develop Implementation Plan – (includes connecting with VSM and AOP's)
- Reconcile Operations Excellence improvements   with Bridge statement
- Safety risk assessments
- Quality defect Pareto analysis / Develop QCP
- Formalized training program
- Benchmarking

- 5S
- LDMS
- Continuous Flow
- Standard Work
- Skills Versatility
- Pull
- Quick Change Over
- Quality at Source
- TPM
- Ergonomics Improvement Plan
- ACP (5-day change event)
- Create value stream focused management structure

FIGURE 30

Phase Two - Traditional Operations Excellence Implementation Model

Phase 3: Succeeding (Process Capability-

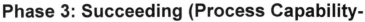

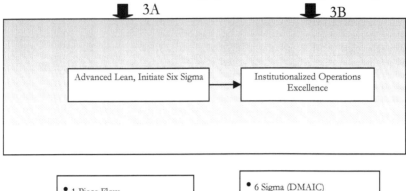

3A	3B
Advanced Lean, Initiate Six Sigma	Institutionalized Operations Excellence

• 1 Piece Flow	• 6 Sigma (DMAIC)
•Production flexing to Takt	• Extending the VS to suppliers
• Mixed Model Level Loading	• PFMEA's performed on existing critical processes
• Process Capability/Six Sigma initiatives	•Safety implementation plan
• Line Stop	• Adherence to NPD process
	• IT Infrastructure Supports Operational Excellence
	• Modular Design
	• Value Stream Accounting

FIGURE 31

Phase Three - Traditional Operations Excellence Implementation Model

Phase 4: Leading (Pursue Perfection)

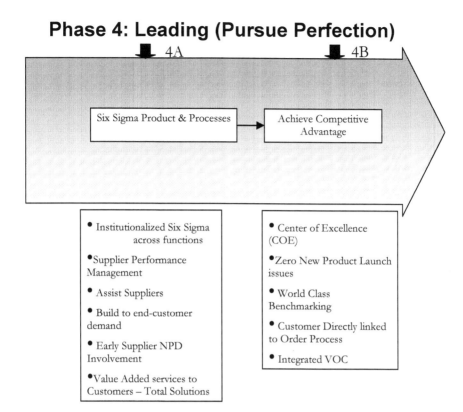

FIGURE 32

Phase Four - Traditional Operations Excellence Implementation Model

Phase 1: Learn (Organizational

| Forces of -- | Customer Expectatio | Situation Analysis | Steering Team |

- Leadership understanding of organizational development and culture change
- Baseline assessment

- Customer Expectations
- Business Expectations

- Business knowledge
- Change leadership
- Establish the need for change

- SWOT
- Leadership of change
- Communication plan
- Establish urgency
- Establish "Why" change

FIGURE 33

Phase One – New Operations Excellence Transformation Model

Phase 1: Learn (Organizational Understanding)

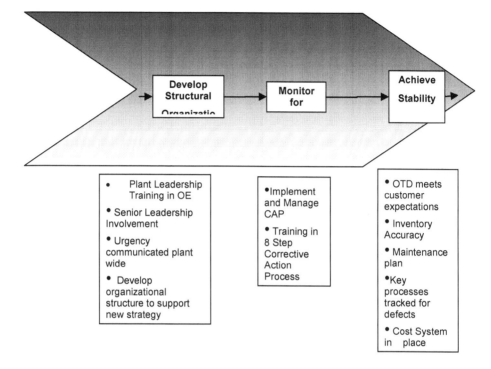

FIGURE 33

Phase One (con't) – New Operations Excellence Transformation Model

Phase 2: Focus (Focused Transformation)

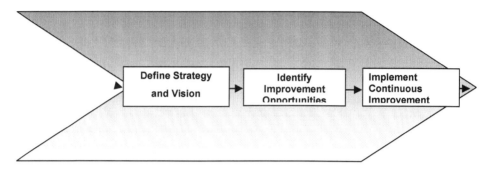

| Define Strategy and Vision | Identify Improvement Opportunities | Implement Continuous Improvement |

•Vision

•Leadership training and development plan

•Communication plan

•Leadership commitment & trust

•Policies and procedures

•Organizational structure

•Organizational effectiveness awareness

•LDMS

•Establish teams

•Facilitators

•Critical thinking

• Create VSM - Order fulfillment

•Current

•Future

•Ideal

• 7 Types of Waste

• Policy Deployment

•Develop Implementation Plan – (includes connecting with VSM and AOP's)

•Safety risk assessments

• Quality defect Pareto analysis / Develop QCP

• Formalized training program

• Benchmarking

•5S

• LDMS

• Continuous Flow

• Standard Work

• Skills Versatility

• Pull

• Quick Change Over

•Quality at Source

• TPM

•Ergonomics Improvement Plan

• Visual Leadership and communication

• ACP (5-day change event)

• Create value stream focused management structure

FIGURE 34

Phase Two – New Operations Excellence Transformation Model

Phase 3: Align (Structure to Engage)

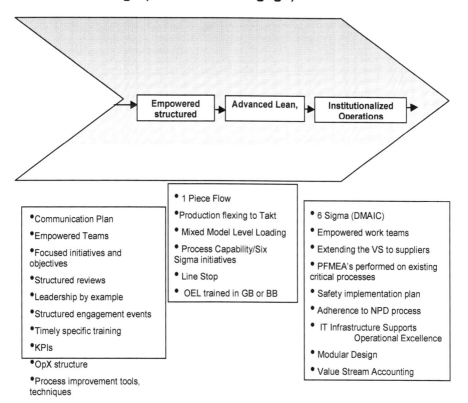

| Empowered structured | Advanced Lean, | Institutionalized Operations |

- •Communication Plan
- •Empowered Teams
- •Focused initiatives and objectives
- •Structured reviews
- •Leadership by example
- •Structured engagement events
- •Timely specific training
- •KPIs
- •OpX structure
- •Process improvement tools, techniques

- • 1 Piece Flow
- •Production flexing to Takt
- • Mixed Model Level Loading
- • Process Capability/Six Sigma initiatives
- • Line Stop
- • OEL trained in GB or BB

- • 6 Sigma (DMAIC)
- • Empowered work teams
- • Extending the VS to suppliers
- • PFMEA's performed on existing critical processes
- • Safety implementation plan
- • Adherence to NPD process
- • IT Infrastructure Supports Operational Excellence
- • Modular Design
- • Value Stream Accounting

FIGURE 35

Phase Three – New Operations Excellence Transformation Model

Phase 4: Sustain (Institutional Culture)

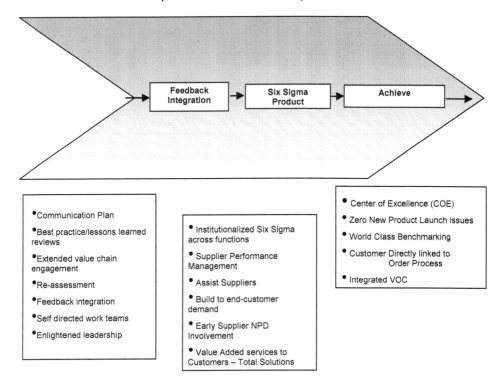

FIGURE 36

Phase Four – New Operations Excellence Transformation Model

Made in the USA
Lexington, KY
24 January 2012